Mastering Postman

A Comprehensive Guide to Building End-to-End APIs with Testing, Integration and Automation

Oliver James

Published by: GitforGits
Publisher: Sonal Dhandre
www.gitforgits.com
support@gitforgits.com

Printed in India

First Printing: April 2023

ISBN: 978-8119177073

Cover Design by: Kitten Publishing

Content

Preface

"Mastering Postman" is the ultimate guide for anyone looking to streamline their API development process. Whether you're a seasoned developer or just starting out, this book will take you through every step of the API lifecycle and equip you with the knowledge and tools you need to create better APIs faster.

Starting with API design, the book covers the best practices for creating APIs that are intuitive, easy to use, and scalable. You'll learn how to use Postman to test your APIs thoroughly and ensure they're working as intended before deploying them. The book then delves into API documentation and mocking, showing you how to create comprehensive documentation that's easy to understand and use. You'll also learn how to use Postman to mock your APIs, allowing you to test your code in a safe environment before deploying it to production. With a focus on Python, Flask, and JavaScript coding, "Mastering Postman" teaches you how to build APIs that are powerful, efficient, and easy to use. You'll also learn about API governance, integration, publishing, and the Postman CLI.

Throughout the book, you'll find practical examples and real-world scenarios that demonstrate how to apply the concepts you learn to your own projects. You'll also find tips and tricks to help you become more productive and efficient as you work on your APIs. Whether you're a developer, a product manager, or a technical writer, "Mastering Postman" will give you the skills and knowledge you need to create APIs that are robust, reliable, and easy to use. With this book as your guide, you'll be able to streamline your API development process and deliver better APIs faster than ever before.

In this book you will learn how to:

- **Streamline API development process with Postman for faster delivery.**
- Learn API design, testing, documentation, and mocking with real-world examples.
- Build APIs using Python, Flask, and JavaScript for better performance.
- Master API governance, integration, and publishing with Postman.
- Leverage Postman CLI for advanced API testing and automation.
- Collaborate efficiently using Postman collections, environments, and workspaces.

GitforGits

Prerequisites

Mastering Postman is ideal for developers and software engineers who want to build end-to-end APIs efficiently and effectively. It is suitable for both beginners who are new to API development and experienced developers who want to master their skills in API development, testing, debugging and integration.

Before reading this book, you should have a basic understanding of web development, HTTP protocol, and API concepts.

Codes Usage

Are you in need of some helpful code examples to assist you in your programming and documentation? Look no further! Our book offers a wealth of supplemental material, including code examples and exercises.

Not only is this book here to aid you in getting your job done, but you have our permission to use the example code in your programs and documentation. However, please note that if you are reproducing a significant portion of the code, we do require you to contact us for permission.

But don't worry, using several chunks of code from this book in your program or answering a question by citing our book and quoting example code does not require permission. But if you do choose to give credit, an attribution typically includes the title, author, publisher, and ISBN. For example, "Mastering Postman by Oliver James".

If you are unsure whether your intended use of the code examples falls under fair use or the permissions outlined above, please do not hesitate to reach out to us at kittenpub.kdp@gmail.com.

We are happy to assist and clarify any concerns.

Acknowledgement

I would like to express my heartfelt gratitude to Pravin Dhandre and the entire team at GitforGits for their invaluable contribution towards the successful completion of my book "Mastering Postman." Without their expertise, dedication, and unwavering support, this book would not have been possible.

Pravin Dhandre, the founder of GitforGits, played a pivotal role in the book's development, providing technical guidance, support, and encouragement at every step of the way. His vast knowledge and experience in API testing, combined with his passion for teaching, made him an indispensable partner in this project. I would like to extend my deepest appreciation to Pravin for his unwavering commitment and invaluable contribution to this book. I would also like to thank the GitforGits team for their exceptional work in reviewing, editing, and providing feedback on the book's content. Their attention to detail and commitment to excellence helped ensure that the book is of the highest quality and meets the needs of readers.

Finally, I would like to express my gratitude to my family and colleagues at my workplace for their unwavering support and understanding throughout the writing process. Their encouragement, patience, and love gave me the strength and motivation to keep going, even when the going got tough.

In particular, I would like to thank my wife, Jane, and my children, Emily and James, for their unconditional love and support. Their unwavering belief in me and my abilities has been the driving force behind this project, and I could not have done it without them.

To my colleagues at my workplace, thank you for your support and encouragement throughout this journey. Your feedback, suggestions, and ideas were invaluable in shaping the content of this book, and I am deeply grateful for your contributions.

CHAPTER 1: API LIFECYCLE AND POSTMAN

API, or Application Programming Interface, is a set of rules and protocols that allows different software applications to communicate and exchange data with each other. Essentially, an API acts as an intermediary between two different software applications, allowing them to interact with each other in a standardized and secure manner. APIs have become increasingly important in today's digital transformation and software development landscape. With the rise of cloud computing and mobile technologies, there has been a growing need for software applications to communicate with each other seamlessly, regardless of the platforms or devices they are running on. APIs provide a way for applications to achieve this level of integration by providing a standardized way to exchange data and functionality.

One of the key benefits of APIs is that they allow organizations to unlock the value of their data and functionality, by exposing them to external developers and partners. By providing APIs, organizations can make their data and functionality available to other applications and services, creating new opportunities for innovation and collaboration. For example, a bank could expose APIs that allow developers to build financial applications that integrate with the bank's core services, such as account management or payment processing.

APIs also provide a way for organizations to improve the agility and scalability of their software systems. By decoupling the front-end and back-end components of an application, APIs allow organizations to make changes to one component without impacting the other. This can help to reduce the risk of downtime or system failures, while also allowing organizations to quickly adapt to changing business needs.

Another important benefit of APIs is that they can help to improve the user experience of software applications. By providing access to data and functionality from multiple sources, APIs can help to create more personalized and context-aware applications. For example, an e-commerce application could use APIs to integrate with a customer's social media accounts, to provide personalized product recommendations based on their interests and preferences.

Understanding API Lifecycle

Understanding the complete lifecycle of an API is crucial for successful API development and management. The lifecycle includes several stages, starting with the design phase, where API architects determine the requirements for the API and create the API specification. Next, developers build the API and test it before releasing it for production use. After release, the API must be managed and monitored to ensure it meets the required service level agreements (SLAs) and performs optimally. Finally, the API may be retired, requiring developers to plan for and execute a smooth transition for any dependent systems or applications. By understanding each stage of the API lifecycle, developers can ensure their APIs meet the needs of the end-users while providing a positive experience.

Following are the 7 stages of the lifecycle of any API:
1. API Design
2. API Development
3. API Testing
4. API Deployment
5. API Monitoring
6. API Versioning
7. API Retirement

API Design

API design is the first stage in the lifecycle of an API. This stage involves identifying the use case of the API, defining the API endpoints and methods, creating a request and response schema, and documenting the API using OpenAPI or similar tools. The API design process should also take into consideration factors such as security, scalability, and ease of use for developers who will be using the API. During the design process, the API developer should collaborate with other stakeholders, such as product owners, UX designers, and other developers, to ensure that the API meets the requirements of the business and end-users.

API Development

Once the API design is complete, the next stage is API development. This stage involves writing backend code to support the API, creating and configuring a local server, handling authentication and authorization, and building and testing endpoints in Postman or similar tools. The API developer should ensure that the code is well-organized, modular, and adheres to best practices in coding standards. The developer should also conduct unit testing and integration testing to ensure that the API functions as expected.

API Testing

API testing is an essential stage in the lifecycle of an API. This stage involves testing the API for different scenarios, such as positive and negative tests, error handling, and load testing. The API developer should also conduct security testing to identify and address potential security vulnerabilities. Postman can be used to automate API testing, making it easier for developers to run and repeat tests quickly and efficiently.

API Deployment

API deployment is the stage where the API is made available for use by external users. This stage involves deploying the API to a production environment, configuring the API gateway, and configuring API security. The API developer should ensure that the API deployment is well-documented and that there is a clear process for deploying updates or fixes to the API.

API Monitoring

API monitoring is an essential stage in the lifecycle of an API. This stage involves monitoring the API for performance and availability, detecting and troubleshooting issues, and identifying potential security threats. The API developer should use tools such as Postman's monitoring capabilities to track API performance and identify potential issues that may arise.

API Versioning

As an API evolves over time, there may be a need for versioning to ensure that older versions of the API continue to function as expected. This stage involves maintaining and managing multiple versions of the API, ensuring backward compatibility, and communicating changes to API users. The API developer should use tools such as Postman to manage API versioning and ensure that changes are communicated clearly to users.

API Retirement

API retirement is the final stage in the lifecycle of an API. This stage involves retiring an older version of the API and communicating the retirement to API users. The API developer should ensure that the API documentation is updated to reflect the retirement and provide guidance on migrating to a newer version of the API.

To sum it up, the complete lifecycle of an API involves several stages, each with its own set of tasks and considerations. By understanding and following the complete lifecycle of an API, API developers can ensure that their APIs are designed, developed, tested, deployed, monitored, versioned, and retired in a well-organized and efficient manner. This can help to ensure that the APIs meet the needs of the business and end-users, while also maintaining security, performance, and scalability. Additionally, following the complete lifecycle of an API can help API developers to build trust with API users, by providing clear and consistent communication throughout the entire process. Ultimately, by understanding the complete lifecycle of an API and following best practices at each stage, API developers can create high-quality APIs that meet the needs of the business and end-users, while also providing a positive experience for API users.

Introduction to Postman

Postman is a versatile API development tool that simplifies the process of creating and testing APIs. It provides an intuitive graphical user interface that allows developers to design, test, and document APIs with ease. Postman is widely used by software developers, testers, and DevOps engineers to streamline the software development process, automate testing, and improve collaboration. It supports a variety of APIs, including REST and SOAP, and provides powerful features for creating request and response schemas, generating code snippets, and collaborating with team members. With Postman, developers can accelerate their development workflows, ensure the quality of their APIs, and improve their overall productivity.

Postman's Capabilities

Postman is a powerful tool that allows developers to design, test, and debug APIs, as well as to create and publish API documentation. The given below are some of the key features of Postman:

API Design and Mocking

Developers can use Postman to design APIs by creating requests and responses, defining endpoints, and setting up mock servers to simulate API behavior. This enables developers to experiment with different endpoints and data structures without needing a fully functional backend. With Postman, developers can quickly iterate on their API design and ensure that it's working as expected.

Testing and Debugging

Postman provides developers with the ability to test and debug APIs in real time, allowing them to send requests and receive responses as they build their API. This makes testing and debugging much easier and faster. Postman offers a comprehensive array of testing capabilities, including automated testing, integration testing, and load testing, amongst others.

API Documentation

Postman enables developers to create and publish API documentation that can be shared with other users. The documentation contains in-depth explanations of each endpoint, as well as the request and response formats and any other pertinent information. This documentation helps other developers understand how to use the API and saves time by addressing common questions.

Collaboration

Postman is designed to make it easier for developers to work together. It offers a variety of collaboration features, such as sharing API collections, test results, and other data. Additionally, Postman provides version control, which allows developers to monitor any changes made to APIs over time, keeping track of who made the changes and when.

Automation

Postman offers a wide range of automation features that can be used by developers to automate routine tasks such as testing, documentation, and deployment. For example, developers can use Postman to set up automated tests for their API, automatically generate documentation, and deploy changes to their API with a single click.

To sum it up, Postman is an essential tool for any developer working with APIs. With its powerful API design and mocking capabilities, testing and debugging features, comprehensive documentation, collaboration tools, and automation capabilities, Postman can save developers time and effort while improving the quality and functionality of their APIs.

Applications of Postman

Postman is a flexible tool that can be utilized in a wide variety of settings and contexts due to its adaptability. The following are some of the most important applications:

- Postman is a tool that is frequently utilized by developers for the purposes of designing, testing, and documenting APIs. It simplifies the process of developing APIs by providing a variety of features, such as automated testing and mocking, which are provided by it.
- Testing an API can also be automated with the help of Postman, which is used by testers. Testers are afforded the opportunity to create test suites, to define test cases, and to automatically run tests.
- Postman is becoming an increasingly popular tool for automating DevOps-related tasks like testing, documentation, and deployment in environments where DevOps is practiced. It is compatible with a wide variety of DevOps tools, such as Git, Jenkins, and Docker, among others.

In a nutshell, Postman gives developers access to a variety of features that make it easier for them to manage the entire API development lifecycle, from the design phase to the testing phase to the deployment phase. Postman is an essential and helpful tool in the field of software development because it streamlines the development process, enhances testing, makes collaboration easier, and integrates with a variety of other tools.

Install and Configure Postman

This is a step-by-step walkthrough on how to install and configure Postman on your computer. They are:

Download Postman

- Go to the official Postman website: https://www.postman.com/downloads/

- Choose the version appropriate for your operating system (Windows, macOS, or Linux).

- Click the "Download" button and wait for the download to finish.

Install Postman

- Locate the downloaded installation file in your downloads folder or wherever you saved it.

- Double-click the installation file to start the installation process.

- Follow the on-screen instructions to complete the installation.

Launch Postman

- After installation is complete, find the Postman application in your Start menu (Windows) or Applications folder (macOS) or menu (Linux).

- Click on the Postman icon to open the application.

Create/Sign-In Postman Account

When you first launch Postman, you'll see a sign-in prompt. If you already have a Postman account, sign in with your credentials. If you don't have an account, click "Create Account" and follow the prompts to set up your new account.

Configure Postman

- Once you're signed in, you'll see the main Postman interface. On the left-hand side, you'll see a sidebar with a "Collections" tab. Collections are used to organize and group your API requests.

- Click the "+" button next to "Collections" to create a new collection. Give your collection a name and an optional description, then click "Create".

- With your new collection selected, click the "+" button next to the "Tabs" section at the top of the interface. This will open a new tab for creating an API request.

- In the new request tab, choose the appropriate HTTP method (GET, POST, PUT, etc.) for your request from the dropdown menu to the left of the URL input field.

- Enter the URL for your API endpoint in the URL input field.

- If your request requires headers, click the "Headers" tab below the URL input field and add the necessary key-value pairs.

- If your request requires a payload (for example, a POST or PUT request), click the "Body" tab below the URL input field and select the appropriate format (such as "raw" or "form-data") to input your data.

- Once you've configured your request, click the blue "Send" button on the right side of the URL input field to send the request to the API endpoint. The response from the API will appear in the lower section of the interface.

You have successfully installed Postman and configured it for your first API request. With Postman, you can now easily make API requests, test and validate API responses, and even document your APIs.

Create New API Project

To create a new API project in Postman, you need to set up a new workspace, create an API specification, and add requests for each endpoint. First, create a new workspace for your project. Then, create a new collection and add requests for each endpoint in your API. Finally, define the request and response schemas for each endpoint using examples, and validate your API's behavior against the defined schemas using Postman's "Test" feature.

Create New Workspace

- In the top-right corner of the Postman interface, click on the workspace dropdown (it will show the name of your current workspace).

- Click the "Create New" button at the bottom of the dropdown menu.

- In the "Create New Workspace" dialog, enter a name and an optional description for your new workspace. Choose a visibility setting (public or private) and click "Create Workspace".

Create API Specification

- In your new workspace, click the "APIs" tab in the left sidebar.

- Click the "Create an API" button in the center of the screen.

- In the "New API" dialog, provide a name and an optional description for your API.

- Choose an API schema type. For most cases, you'll want to select "OpenAPI (formerly Swagger) 3.0". Click "Create API" to proceed.

- Postman will now display the API schema editor with a default schema template. Modify the template according to your API requirements. The schema is written in YAML or JSON format, and it describes your API's endpoints, parameters, request bodies, responses, and other details. You can find the OpenAPI 3.0 specification documentation at https://swagger.io/specification/.

Add Requests for Each Endpoint

- In the left sidebar, click the "Collections" tab.

- Click the "+" button next to "Collections" to create a new collection. Give your collection a name and an optional description, then click "Create".

- With your new collection selected, click the "Add a request" button (it looks like a "+" inside a circle) next to your collection's name.

- In the "New Request" dialog, enter a name for your request, choose a method (GET, POST, PUT, etc.), and click "Save to [Your Collection Name]".

- In the new request tab, enter the URL for your API endpoint in the URL input field.

- Configure headers, query parameters, or request bodies as needed for your endpoint.

- Repeat steps 3c-3f for each endpoint in your API.

Test API Endpoints

- With an API request tab open, click the blue "Send" button on the right side of the

URL input field to send the request to the API endpoint.

- The response from the API will appear in the lower section of the interface. Review the response status, headers, and body to ensure the request was successful and the API is functioning as expected.

- You can create test scripts for your requests by clicking on the "Tests" tab below the URL input field. Postman uses JavaScript (specifically the pm object) to write and run tests.

For example, to check if the response status is 200, you can write the following test:

```
pm.test("Status code is 200", function () {
    pm.response.to.have.status(200);
});
```

Save API Project

As you work on your API project, Postman automatically saves your changes. Do not forget to periodically click the "Save" button in the top-right corner of the request tab to ensure your work is saved.

By following the steps outlined, you've successfully created a new API project in Postman. You now have a dedicated workspace where you can manage your API requests and collections. Additionally, you've defined an API specification that outlines your endpoints, their inputs, and expected outputs. You've created a collection of requests that allow you to test your endpoints and ensure they're functioning as expected.

Explore Postman's Interface

we'll explore the Postman interface and learn how to navigate through its various components. The interface is designed to provide an efficient and intuitive experience for users, with easy access to all of the features you need.

Main Interface Components

The Postman interface includes several main components such as the sidebar, header bar, request pane, response pane, and tabs. These components help users navigate and interact with the application, making it easier to create and manage API requests. Let us look into each in detail:

Header. The header is located at the very top of the interface. It includes the Postman logo, search bar, workspace switcher, environment switcher, import button, new button, runner button, and account-related controls (such as profile and settings).

Sidebar. The sidebar is located on the left side of the interface. It consists of three main tabs: History, Collections, and APIs. These tabs allow you to access your recent requests, saved collections, and API specifications.

Request Builder. The request builder is the central part of the interface. It's where you create, configure, and send API requests. It includes the HTTP method selector, URL input, request tabs (Params, Authorization, Headers, Body, Pre-request Script, and Tests), and the Send and Save buttons.

Response Viewer. The response viewer is located below the request builder. It shows the API response when you send a request. It includes the response status, time, size, and tabs for displaying the response body, cookies, headers, and test results.

Header

Search bar. Use the search bar to find requests, collections, environments, or APIs by entering keywords.

Workspace switcher. Click on the workspace dropdown to view, create, or switch between workspaces. Workspaces allow you to organize and collaborate on API projects with team members.

Environment switcher. Click on the environment dropdown to create, edit, or switch between environments. Environments are sets of key-value pairs that can be used as variables in your requests.

Import button: Click on the "Import" button to import API specifications, requests, or collections from various sources, such as files or URLs.

New button: Click on the "New" button to create a new request, collection, environment, API, or mock server.

Runner button: Click on the "Runner" button to open the collection runner, which allows you to run a series of requests with specific configurations, such as iterations and data files.

Account-related controls: Click on your profile picture to access your account settings, billing, and other options.

Sidebar

History tab: Click on the "History" tab to view a list of your recent requests. You can filter requests by date or method and search for specific requests.

Collections tab: Click on the "Collections" tab to view your saved collections. Collections are groups of related requests, which can be organized into folders. To create a new collection, click the "+" button next to "Collections". To add a request to a collection, click the "Add a request" button (it looks like a "+" inside a circle) next to a collection's name.

APIs tab: Click on the "APIs" tab to view your saved API specifications. API specifications describe the endpoints, parameters, request bodies, responses, and other details of your APIs. To create a new API, click the "Create an API" button in the center of the screen.

Request Builder

HTTP method selector: Click on the dropdown menu to the left of the URL input field to choose the appropriate HTTP method (GET, POST, PUT, DELETE, etc.) for your request.

URL input: Type the URL for your API endpoint in the URL input field. You can use variables, such as {{base_url}} or {{api_key}}, which will be replaced with their corresponding values from the selected environment or global variables.

Params tab: Click on the "Params" tab to add or edit query parameters for your request. Postman will automatically append these parameters to the URL.

Authorization tab: Click on the "Authorization" tab to set up authentication for your request. Postman supports various authentication types, such as Basic Auth, OAuth 2.0, API Key, and Bearer Token. Select the appropriate type and provide the required information.

Headers tab: Click on the "Headers" tab to add or edit headers for your request. Headers can be used to provide additional information to the server, such as content type or authentication data.

Body tab: Click on the "Body" tab to add a request body, which is required for some HTTP methods like POST and PUT. You can choose between different body types, such as raw, form-data, x-www-form-urlencoded, or binary.

Pre-request Script tab: Click on the "Pre-request Script" tab to write JavaScript code that will run before sending the request. You can use this feature to set up variables, make additional API calls, or perform other tasks.

Tests tab: Click on the "Tests" tab to write test scripts for your request. Postman uses JavaScript (specifically the pm object) to write and run tests. This allows you to assert that your API behaves as expected, returning correct status codes, response bodies, and more.

Send button: Click on the blue "Send" button to send the request to the API endpoint

Save button: Click on the "Save" button to save your request to a collection or update an existing request in a collection. Remember to save your work periodically to avoid losing any changes.

Response Viewer

Status: The response status is displayed at the top left of the response viewer, showing the HTTP status code and a brief description.

Time: The time taken for the API to respond is displayed next to the status. This can be helpful for identifying performance issues.

Size: The size of the response, including headers and body, is displayed next to the time.

Response Body tab: Click on the "Body" tab to view the API response body. You can choose between different formats, such as Pretty, Raw, and Preview. Postman will attempt to display the response in the most readable format, based on the content type.

Cookies tab: Click on the "Cookies" tab to view any cookies sent with the response.

Headers tab: Click on the "Headers" tab to view the response headers. These can provide important information about the server, content type, and other metadata.

Test Results tab: Click on the "Test Results" tab to view the results of any test scripts that ran with the request. Successful tests will be displayed in green, while failed tests will be in red. You can use this information to debug issues with your API or validate its behavior.

By understanding the various components of the Postman interface and how to navigate through them, you'll be better equipped to design, build, test, and document APIs effectively. With practice, you'll become more proficient in utilizing Postman's features to streamline your API development process.

Additional Features and Tools

In the previous section, we've covered the main components of the Postman interface, but there are additional features and tools that can enhance your API development workflow:

Environments and Variables

Environments: These are sets of key-value pairs that can be used as variables in your requests. To create a new environment, click the environment dropdown in the top-right corner of the interface, and then click "Manage Environments". In the "Manage Environments" window, click "Add" to create a new environment, enter the key-value pairs, and save your changes.

Global Variables: These are key-value pairs that are available across all environments. You can create and manage global variables by clicking on the gear icon in the top-right corner of the interface and selecting "Globals".

Using Variables: To use a variable in a request, enclose the variable name in double curly braces, like {{variable_name}}. Postman will replace the variable with its corresponding value when the request is sent.

Mock Servers

Mock servers allow you to simulate API endpoints without the need for an actual backend server. This can be helpful for testing and development purposes. To create a mock server, click the "New" button in the top-right corner of the interface and select "Mock Server".

Monitors

Monitors allow you to schedule your API requests to run automatically at regular intervals. This can be useful for monitoring the health of your APIs or performing scheduled tasks. To create a monitor, click the "New" button in the top-right corner of the interface and select "Monitor".

API Documentation

Postman can automatically generate documentation for your APIs based on your collections and API specifications. To generate documentation, click on the three-dot menu next to a collection in the Collections tab and select "Publish Docs" or "View in Web". You can customize the appearance, add descriptions, and include examples for your documentation.

Collaboration and Sharing

Postman offers various collaboration features to help teams work together on API projects.

Team Workspaces: You can create and share workspaces with team members, allowing everyone to access the same collections, environments, and APIs.

Sharing Collections: To share a collection with your team or the public, click on the three-dot menu next to the collection in the Collections tab and select "Share". You can also generate a shareable link or embed a Run in Postman button on your website.

Comments: You can leave comments on requests and collections to discuss changes or ask questions. To add a comment, click on the comment icon next to a request or collection's name.

Integrations

Postman offers various integrations with third-party services, such as GitHub, GitLab, Bitbucket, and others. These integrations can help you automate tasks and streamline your API development workflow. To explore available integrations, click on your profile picture in the top-right corner of the interface and select "Integrations".

Postman is a versatile tool that offers a wide range of features and functionalities. As you continue to use it, you will uncover more of its capabilities, allowing you to customize and tailor your workflow to your specific needs.

CHAPTER 2: API DESIGN

Principles of API Design

API design is a crucial aspect of building a successful API. A well-designed API is easy to understand, maintain, and extend. The given below are some key principles of API design, along with examples to illustrate each principle:

Apply Consistent and Meaningful Naming

Use consistent naming conventions for resources, endpoints, and parameters. Choose descriptive names that clearly represent the purpose or functionality of each component.

Example:
- Good: /users/{user_id}/orders
- Bad: /u/{user_id}/o

Embrace RESTful Principles

REST (Representational State Transfer) is an architectural style for designing networked applications. It emphasizes statelessness, cacheability, and a clear separation of concerns between client and server. Some key RESTful principles include:
- Use HTTP methods (GET, POST, PUT, DELETE) to represent actions on resources.
- Use resource-based URLs (e.g., /users, /orders) instead of action-based URLs (e.g., /getUser, /createOrder).
- Return meaningful HTTP status codes to indicate the result of an operation (e.g., 200 OK, 201 Created, 400 Bad Request, 404 Not Found).

Example:
- List all users: GET /users
- Create a new user: POST /users
- Update an existing user: PUT /users/{user_id}
- Delete a user: DELETE /users/{user_id}

Use JSON for Request and Response Bodies

JSON (JavaScript Object Notation) is a lightweight and human-readable data interchange format. It is widely used for APIs because of its simplicity and ease of use. Use JSON for both request and response bodies, and set the Content-Type and Accept headers accordingly.

Example:

```json
{
  "name": "John Doe",
  "email": "john.doe@example.com"
}
```

Version the API

As your API evolves, you may need to introduce breaking changes. To avoid disrupting existing clients, use versioning in your API. This can be done through the URL, headers, or other means.

Example:
- Include the version in the URL: /api/v1/users
- Use a custom header: X-API-Version: 1

Support Pagination, Filtering, and Sorting

APIs often return large sets of data. To improve performance and usability, support pagination, filtering, and sorting for your API endpoints.

Example:
- Pagination: /users?limit=10&page=2
- Filtering: /users?status=active
- Sorting: /users?sort=name,-created_at

Do Clear and Comprehensive Documentation

Clear and comprehensive documentation is essential for API users. Provide detailed information on each endpoint, including the URL, method, parameters, request and response formats, and examples. Consider using tools like Swagger or Postman to generate interactive documentation.

Implement Proper Authentication and Authorization

Secure your API by implementing proper authentication and authorization. Choose an appropriate authentication method, such as OAuth 2.0, API keys, or JWT tokens. Ensure that users can only access the resources and perform the actions they are authorized to do.

Example:
- OAuth 2.0: Use an access token to authenticate requests: Authorization: Bearer

<access_token>
- API Key: Include the API key in the header or query parameter: X-API-Key: <api_key> or ?api_key=<api_key>

By following these principles, you can design APIs that are easy to understand, maintain, and extend.

Define API Endpoints

API endpoints are the specific points at which an API interacts with a server to perform certain actions, such as retrieving, updating, or deleting data. Each endpoint is a combination of the URL path and the HTTP method used to perform the action. In the context of APIs, an endpoint can be thought of as a single function or operation that the API exposes for use by clients.

An API is a collection of endpoints, data structures, and protocols that enable developers to create applications that can communicate with other systems, services, or components. In summary, an API is a collection of endpoints, while an endpoint is a specific point of interaction within the API.

REST API (Representational State Transfer) is an architectural style for designing networked applications. RESTful APIs use standard HTTP methods and resource-based URLs to perform actions on resources. The principles of RESTful API design encourage simplicity, scalability, and maintainability.

REST API Endpoints

Retrieve a list of users:
Method: GET
Endpoint: /api/v1/users

Create a new user:
Method: POST
Endpoint: /api/v1/users

Retrieve a specific user by ID:
Method: GET
Endpoint: /api/v1/users/{user_id}

Update a user's information:
Method: PUT
Endpoint: /api/v1/users/{user_id}

Delete a user:
Method: DELETE
Endpoint: /api/v1/users/{user_id}

SOAP (Simple Object Access Protocol) is a protocol for exchanging structured information in the implementation of web services. SOAP relies on XML for its message format and typically uses HTTP or HTTPS for transport. Unlike REST, which is an architectural style, SOAP is a specific protocol with strict rules and standards.

SOAP APIs define operations (similar to endpoints in REST) in a WSDL (Web Services Description Language) file, which is an XML-based language for describing the functionality offered by a web service. Clients can parse the WSDL to generate code for interacting with the SOAP API.

SOAP API Operations (Endpoints)

Retrieve a list of users:
Operation: GetUsers
SOAP Action: http://example.com/GetUsers

Sample SOAP Request:

```xml
<soapenv:Envelope
xmlns:soapenv="http://schemas.xmlsoap.org/soap/envelope/"
xmlns:web="http://example.com/">
  <soapenv:Header/>
  <soapenv:Body>
    <web:GetUsers/>
  </soapenv:Body>
</soapenv:Envelope>
```

Create a new user:
Operation: CreateUser

SOAP Action: http://example.com/CreateUser

Sample SOAP Request:

```
<soapenv:Envelope
xmlns:soapenv="http://schemas.xmlsoap.org/soap/envelope/"
xmlns:web="http://example.com/">
  <soapenv:Header/>
  <soapenv:Body>
   <web:CreateUser>
     <web:name>John Doe</web:name>
     <web:email>john.doe@example.com</web:email>
   </web:CreateUser>
  </soapenv:Body>
</soapenv:Envelope>
```

Overall, API endpoints (or operations in the case of SOAP) are the specific points of interaction within an API, where clients can perform actions on resources.

Write API Endpoints with Python and Flask

There are several methods to write API endpoints, depending on the programming language and framework you choose. Some popular languages and frameworks for writing API endpoints include:

1. Python with Flask or Django
2. JavaScript with Node.js and Express.js
3. Ruby with Ruby on Rails
4. Java with Spring Boot
5. PHP with Laravel or Symfony

In this section, we'll learn how to write an API endpoint using Python and Flask, a lightweight and flexible web framework. To get started, make sure you have Python installed and follow these steps:

Install Flask

Open your terminal or command prompt and run the following command to install Flask:

pip install Flask

Create New Python File

Create a new Python file, e.g., app.py, in a new directory for your project.

Write Flask Application

Open app.py and write the following code to create a simple Flask application with one API endpoint:

```python
from flask import Flask, jsonify

app = Flask(__name__)

@app.route('/api/users', methods=['GET'])
def get_users():
    users = [
        {'id': 1, 'name': 'John Doe', 'email': 'john.doe@example.com'},
        {'id': 2, 'name': 'Jane Doe', 'email': 'jane.doe@example.com'}
    ]
    return jsonify(users)

if __name__ == '__main__':
    app.run(debug=True)
```

This code defines a simple Flask application with one API endpoint, /api/users, that responds to GET requests. The get_users function returns a JSON array of user objects. The jsonify function from Flask is used to convert the Python list of dictionaries into a JSON response.

Run the Flask Application

In your terminal or command prompt, navigate to the directory containing app.py and run the following command:

```
python app.py
```

This will start the Flask development server on port 5000.

Test the API Endpoint

Open your web browser or a tool like Postman and navigate to the following URL:

```
http://localhost:5000/api/users
```

You should see a JSON response containing the list of users:

```
[
    {"id": 1, "name": "John Doe", "email": "john.doe@example.com"},
    {"id": 2, "name": "Jane Doe", "email": "jane.doe@example.com"}
]
```

This is a simple demonstration of how to write an API endpoint using Python and Flask. You can extend this example by adding more endpoints, implementing other HTTP methods (e.g., POST, PUT, DELETE), and connecting to a database for storing and retrieving data.

Create Request and Response Schema

Creating request and response schemas in Postman helps you define the structure of the API request and response, making it easier for other developers to understand and use your API. To create request and response schemas in Postman, you can use the "Examples" feature to define example requests and responses for your API endpoints. The given below is a quick direction on how you can implement:

Open Postman

Open Postman and create a new request or select an existing request in a collection.

Add New Example

Click on the "Examples" button located on the right side of the request's title bar. A dropdown menu will appear, showing any existing examples. To add a new example, click on the "+ Add Example" button in the dropdown menu.

Edit Example's Name

A new tab will open for editing the example. By default, the example's name will be "Untitled Example." You can change the name by clicking on it and entering a new name that describes the example, such as "Get User Success."

Define Request Schema

In the "Request" section of the example, you can define the request schema. This includes the method, URL, headers, query parameters, and body.

Method:

Select the appropriate HTTP method (e.g., GET, POST, PUT, DELETE) from the dropdown menu.

URL:

Enter the URL for the API endpoint. You can use variables, such as {{base_url}}, to make the example more dynamic.

Params:

If your API endpoint requires query parameters, click on the "Params" tab and enter the key-value pairs.

Headers:

If your API endpoint requires specific headers, click on the "Headers" tab and enter the key-value pairs.

Body:

If your API endpoint requires a request body, click on the "Body" tab and choose the appropriate format (e.g., raw, JSON, form-data, x-www-form-urlencoded). Enter the request body content.

Define Response Schema

In the "Response" section of the example, you can define the response schema. This includes the status code, headers, and body.

Status:
Enter the expected HTTP status code for the response (e.g., 200 OK, 201 Created, 400 Bad Request).

Headers:
If your API returns specific headers, click on the "Headers" tab and enter the key-value pairs.

Body:
Click on the "Body" tab and enter the expected response body content. If your response is in JSON format, make sure to write valid JSON.

Save the Example

After defining the request and response schemas, click the "Save" button in the top-right corner of the example tab.

You can create multiple examples for each API request to cover different scenarios, such as successful requests, errors, and edge cases. These examples will be included in your API documentation, making it easier for other developers to understand how to use your API.

Once you've defined the request and response schemas using examples, you can use Postman's "Test" feature to validate your API's behavior against the defined schemas. Additionally, you can use Postman's "Generate Code" feature to generate code snippets in various programming languages, based on the examples you've created.

Document APIs using OpenAPI

OpenAPI is a specification for describing, producing, consuming, and visualizing RESTful web services. Formerly known as Swagger, the OpenAPI Specification (OAS) provides a standardized format for documenting APIs, making it easier for developers to understand and consume them. OpenAPI uses JSON or YAML to describe the API's details, including endpoints, request and response formats, authentication, and more.

Documenting an API involves creating comprehensive, easy-to-understand documentation that describes the API's functionality, endpoints, request and response formats, authentication methods, and any other relevant information. A well-documented API enables developers to quickly understand and integrate with the API, improving the overall developer experience.

To document an API using OpenAPI, you need to create an OpenAPI definition file, which is a JSON or YAML file that follows the OpenAPI Specification. The given below is a step-by-step walkthrough on how to create a simple OpenAPI definition file, along with a sample documentation for a basic API with a single endpoint.

Choose Format (JSON or YAML)

Choose whether you want to use JSON or YAML for your OpenAPI definition file. Both formats are widely supported and easy to work with, but YAML is often considered more human-readable.

Create OpenAPI Definition File

Create a new file with the appropriate extension (.json or .yaml) to store your OpenAPI definition. For this example, we'll create a file called openapi.yaml.

Define Basic API Information

Start by defining the basic information about your API, including the OpenAPI version, API title, description, and version. For example:

```
openapi: 3.0.0
info:
  title: Sample API
  description: A sample API to demonstrate OpenAPI documentation.
  version: 1.0.0
```

Define API Server

Next, define the API server's URL and a brief description.

```
servers:
  - url: https://api.example.com/v1
    description: Production server (uses live data)
```

Define API Endpoints

Now, define your API endpoints, including the path, HTTP method, summary, description, request parameters, and response format. For example, let us define a GET

/users endpoint that retrieves a list of users:

```
paths:
 /users:
  get:
   summary: Get a list of users
   description: Retrieve a list of users with their basic information.
   responses:
    200:
     description: A list of users
     content:
      application/json:
       schema:
        type: array
        items:
         $ref: '#/components/schemas/User'
```

Define Data Models (Schemas)

Define the data models (schemas) used in your API, such as request and response payloads.
In the below sample program, we'll define a simple User schema:

```
components:
 schemas:
  User:
   type: object
   properties:
    id:
     type: integer
     format: int64
     example: 1
    name:
     type: string
```

                example: John Doe
              email:
                type: string
                format: email
                example: john.doe@example.com

The given below is the complete openapi.yaml file for our sample API:

```
openapi: 3.0.0
info:
  title: Sample API
  description: A sample API to demonstrate OpenAPI documentation.
  version: 1.0.0
servers:
  - url: https://api.example.com/v1
    description: Production server (uses live data)
paths:
  /users:
    get:
      summary: Get a list of users
      description: Retrieve a list of users with their basic information.
      responses:
        200:
          description: A list of users
          content:
            application/json:
              schema:
                type: array
                items:
                  $ref: '#/components/schemas/User'
components:
  schemas:
```

```yaml
User:
  type: object
  properties:
    id:
      type: integer
      format: int64
      example: 1
    name:
      type: string
      example: John Doe
    email:
      type: string
      format: email
      example: john.doe@example.com
```

Validate and Test OpenAPI Definition

To validate your OpenAPI definition file, you can use an online validator like the Swagger Editor or a command-line tool like Swagger Inspector. Once your file passes validation, you can use it to generate API documentation automatically using tools like Swagger UI or ReDoc.

Overall, OpenAPI is a powerful tool for documenting APIs, providing a standardized format for describing endpoints, request and response formats, authentication, and more. By following the OpenAPI Specification and using tools like Swagger UI or ReDoc, you can generate comprehensive and easy-to-understand documentation for your API, improving the overall developer experience.

Use Mock Servers for API Design

Mock servers are tools that allow developers to simulate an API without having to build a full backend system. Mock servers can be useful for API design, testing, and development, as they enable developers to experiment with different endpoints and data structures, without the need for a fully functional backend.

Mock servers work by intercepting API requests and returning pre-defined responses that mimic the behavior of a real API. This allows developers to test their code and ensure that it's working as expected, without worrying about the backend implementation. Mock servers can be especially useful for front-end developers, who can use them to develop and test their code independently of the backend development.

In the below given sample illustration, we'll cover how to use a mock server for API design, using the popular tool Mockoon. Mockoon is an open-source mock server that can run on your local machine and is available for Windows, macOS, and Linux.

Install Mockoon

Download and install Mockoon from the official website (https://mockoon.com/). Once installed, launch the application.

Create New Mock Server

Click the "Create a new mock API" button to create a new mock server. Enter a name for your mock server, such as "Sample API," and choose a base URL for your API, such as "http://localhost:3000"

Define API Endpoints

Click the "Add Route" button to define a new API endpoint. Enter the endpoint's path, such as "/users", and choose the HTTP method, such as GET, POST, or PUT.

Define Endpoint's Response

In the endpoint's response tab, you can define the response that the mock server will return when the endpoint is called. This can include a status code, headers, and response body.

For example, let us define a simple response for a GET request to "/users":

Status code: 200 OK
Headers: Content-Type: application/json
Response body:
json
Copy code
{
  "users": [
    {"id": 1, "name": "John Doe", "email": "john.doe@example.com"},

```
  {"id": 2, "name": "Jane Doe", "email": "jane.doe@example.com"}
 ]
}
```

Start Mock Server

Once you've defined your API endpoints and responses, click the "Start" button to start the mock server. This will make your API available at the base URL you defined earlier.

Test the API using Postman

Open Postman and create a new request to your mock API's endpoint, using the base URL you defined earlier (e.g., http://localhost:3000/users).

Send the request and you should see the response that you defined earlier, indicating that your mock API is working as expected.

Mock servers like Mockoon can be incredibly useful for API design, as they enable developers to experiment with different endpoints and data structures, without the need for a fully functional backend. By using mock servers, developers can quickly iterate on their API design and ensure that it's working as expected, without worrying about the backend implementation.

Chapter 3: API Development

Code Backend for API

APIs, or Application Programming Interfaces, are communication interfaces that allow different software applications to exchange information. In a web application, the frontend (client-side) and backend (server-side) are two essential components. The frontend typically involves the user interface and interactions, while the backend is responsible for processing the data and managing communication between the frontend and a database.

The need for backend code to support an API arises from the requirement to facilitate this communication between the frontend and a database. Backend code serves as the intermediary that processes requests, manages the application's data, and implements the business logic. Essentially, it is responsible for:

- Receiving and interpreting API requests from the frontend.
- Executing the required operations to fulfill those requests.
- Accessing and managing the data stored in a database.
- Applying business logic, such as validation and authentication.
- Returning appropriate responses back to the frontend.

In this way, the backend code ensures that the application functions correctly, securely, and efficiently.

Writing Backend Code using Python

Python is a versatile and popular programming language, making it an excellent choice for writing backend code. One widely-used web framework for Python is Flask, which provides a lightweight and easy-to-use platform for building web applications. In this practical solution, we will use Flask to demonstrate how to write backend code for an API.

Install Flask: Begin by installing Flask using pip (Python's package manager). Open your terminal or command prompt and run the following command:

```
pip install Flask
```

Create a new Python file: Name it "app.py" and open it in your preferred text editor.

Set up Flask: Import Flask and create an instance of the Flask class. This instance will be used to define and configure the API.

```
from flask import Flask, jsonify, request
```

```python
app = Flask(__name__)
```

Define a sample dataset: For demonstration purposes, we will create a sample dataset representing a list of books. Each book will have an ID, title, and author.

```python
books = [
    {'id': 1, 'title': 'Book One', 'author': 'Author One'},
    {'id': 2, 'title': 'Book Two', 'author': 'Author Two'},
    {'id': 3, 'title': 'Book Three', 'author': 'Author Three'}
]
```

Create API endpoints: Define the various API endpoints for your application. These endpoints will handle different types of requests, such as getting all books, getting a book by ID, adding a new book, updating a book, and deleting a book.

```python
@app.route('/books', methods=['GET'])
def get_books():
    return jsonify({'books': books})


@app.route('/books/<int:book_id>', methods=['GET'])
def get_book(book_id):
    book = [book for book in books if book['id'] == book_id]
    if not book:
        return jsonify({'error': 'Book not found'}), 404
    return jsonify({'book': book[0]})


@app.route('/books', methods=['POST'])
def add_book():
    new_book = {
        'id': books[-1]['id'] + 1,
        'title': request.json['title'],
        'author': request.json['author']
    }
```

```python
    books.append(new_book)
    return jsonify({'book': new_book}), 201


@app.route('/books/<int:book_id>', methods=['PUT'])
def update_book(book_id):
    book = [book for book in books if book['id'] == book_id]
if not book:
return jsonify({'error': 'Book not found'}), 404
    book[0]['title'] = request.json.get('title', book[0]['title'])
    book[0]['author'] = request.json.get('author', book[0]['author'])
    return jsonify({'book': book[0]})
@app.route('/books/int:book_id', methods=['DELETE'])
def delete_book(book_id):
book = [book for book in books if book['id'] == book_id]
if not book:
return jsonify({'error': 'Book not found'}), 404
    books.remove(book[0])
    return jsonify({'result': 'Book deleted'})
```

Run the Flask application: Add the following lines at the end of your "app.py" file to run the Flask application:

```python
if __name__ == '__main__':
    app.run(debug=True)
```

Save the file and run the following command in your terminal or command prompt:

python app.py

The API should now be running at http://127.0.0.1:5000/.

Test the API: Use Postman to test the API endpoints you created. Send HTTP requests to the various endpoints (e.g., GET, POST, PUT, DELETE) and verify that the API behaves as expected.

This is a simple demonstration of how to write backend code using Python and Flask to support an API. In a real-world application, you would need to implement more advanced features such as error handling, authentication, and connecting to a database. However, this example should provide a solid foundation for understanding the need for backend code to support an API and how to begin writing that code using Python.

Create and Configure Local Server

To create and configure a local server while developing your API using Postman, you can follow these steps:

Install Flask-CORS: When developing an API locally, you may encounter CORS (Cross-Origin Resource Sharing) issues. To handle this, you can use Flask-CORS, an extension that simplifies CORS handling in Flask. Install Flask-CORS using pip:

```
pip install Flask-CORS
```

Modify your Flask application: Open "app.py" and import the CORS class from flask_cors. Then, use the CORS class to enable CORS for your Flask app.

```
from flask import Flask, jsonify, request
from flask_cors import CORS

app = Flask(__name__)
CORS(app)
```

Save your changes and restart your Flask application. Your local server is now configured to handle CORS issues.

Test your API using Postman: Now that your local server is running and configured, you can use Postman to test your API. Open Postman and create a new collection to organize your API requests. For each API endpoint, create a new request in Postman with the appropriate HTTP method (GET, POST, PUT, or DELETE) and URL. Do not forget to replace the base URL (http://127.0.0.1:5000/) with your local server's address.

For example, if you want to test the GET request for all books, create a new GET request in Postman with the following URL:

Click "Send" to send the request to your local server. The server will process the request and return the appropriate response, which will be displayed in Postman. You can view the response's status, headers, and body in the "Response" section of Postman.

Repeat this process for each of your API endpoints, adjusting the HTTP method and URL as needed.

Monitor and debug your local server: As you test your API using Postman, monitor the console output from your Flask application. This can help you identify any issues or errors that may arise during development. If you encounter errors or unexpected behavior, use the debug information provided by Flask to diagnose and fix the issues. You can also use Python's built-in debugger (pdb) or an external debugger like PyCharm to debug your backend code.

Iterate and refine your API: As you develop and test your API using Postman and your local server, you may discover areas for improvement or new functionality to add. Continue refining your API by modifying your backend code, updating your Postman requests, and testing the changes. This iterative process will help you build a robust, well-designed API.

Following these steps, you can create and configure a local server to develop and test your API using Postman. This setup enables you to rapidly iterate on your API, identify issues, and ensure that your backend code functions as expected before deploying it to a production environment.

Manage Authentication and Authorization

Authentication and authorization are essential components of a secure API. Postman makes it easy to test different authentication and authorization methods during development. In this section, we'll cover basic authentication, API keys, and OAuth 2.0.

Testing Basic Authentication

Basic authentication requires a username and password, which are combined and encoded in base64 format, then included in the request's "Authorization" header.

To test basic authentication in Postman:
* Create a new request or select an existing one.

- Go to the "Authorization" tab.
- Select "Basic Auth" from the "Type" dropdown menu.
- Enter the required username and password.
- Postman will automatically generate the "Authorization" header for your request.

Testing API Keys

API keys are unique tokens used to authenticate clients without the need for usernames and passwords. They are often included in the request's headers or as query parameters.

To test API keys in Postman:
- Create a new request or select an existing one.
- Go to the "Authorization" tab.
- Select "API Key" from the "Type" dropdown menu.
- Enter the required key name, key value, and select where the key should be included (header or query parameter).
- Postman will automatically include the API key in your request.

Checking OAuth 2.0

OAuth 2.0 is a widely used authorization framework that enables clients to access protected resources by obtaining an access token. Access tokens are short-lived and must be refreshed using a refresh token.

To test OAuth 2.0 in Postman:
- Create a new request or select an existing one.
- Go to the "Authorization" tab.
- Select "OAuth 2.0" from the "Type" dropdown menu.
- Click "Get New Access Token".
- Fill out the required fields in the "Get New Access Token" dialog, such as Token Name, Grant Type, Callback URL, Auth URL, Access Token URL, Client ID, Client Secret, and Scope. These values depend on the specific API and OAuth provider you're using. Do not forget to check their documentation for the correct values.
- Click "Request Token" to retrieve an access token.
- Once you have the access token, select it from the "Available Tokens" dropdown, and Postman will automatically include it in the "Authorization" header for your request.

Remember that for all these methods, you'll need to implement the corresponding authentication and authorization mechanisms in your backend code. The Flask framework provides several extensions to help with this, such as Flask-HTTPAuth for basic authentication, Flask-Security for API keys, and Flask-OAuthlib for OAuth 2.0.

Write Code for Error Handling

While Postman is primarily used to test APIs and is not meant for writing actual backend code, it can be used to test error handling in your API. By simulating various error scenarios using Postman, you can ensure that your API responds appropriately when errors occur.

To test error handling in your API using Postman, follow these steps:

Implement Error Handling in Backend

Before you can test error handling using Postman, you'll need to implement error handling in your backend code. In the context of the Flask example we've been using, you can utilize Flask's built-in error handling mechanisms.

The given below is an example of how to define a custom error handler in Flask:

```python
from flask import Flask, jsonify

app = Flask(__name__)

@app.errorhandler(404)
def not_found(error):
    return jsonify({'error': 'Not Found'}), 404

@app.errorhandler(400)
def bad_request(error):
    return jsonify({'error': 'Bad Request'}), 400
```

This code defines two custom error handlers for 404 (Not Found) and 400 (Bad Request) errors. When these errors occur, the custom error handlers will return a JSON object with an "error" key describing the error, along with the appropriate HTTP status code.

Simulate Error Scenarios

With error handling implemented in your backend code, you can now use Postman to simulate various error scenarios and test your API's response.

Follow the below steps:
- Create a new request or select an existing one in Postman.
- Modify the request to simulate an error scenario. For example, if you want to test a 404 error, you can change the request URL to an invalid endpoint, like http://127.0.0.1:5000/nonexistent. If you want to test a 400 error, you can send an incomplete or incorrect request body in a POST or PUT request.
- Click "Send" to send the request to your API.
- Examine the response in Postman's "Response" section. Verify that the status code, headers, and body are correct and match the expected error handling behavior.

Refine Error Handling Code

As you test your API's error handling using Postman, you may discover areas for improvement or additional error scenarios to handle. Update your backend code as needed to handle these situations, and continue testing with Postman to ensure that your API responds appropriately to errors.

Just to summarize, implementing error handling in your backend code and testing it using Postman makes easy to build a robust, reliable API that gracefully handles errors and provides useful feedback to clients and thereby create a better user experience and can make your API easier to use and troubleshoot.

Test API Endpoints

To test your API endpoints using Postman, you'll need to create requests for each endpoint and verify that they return the expected responses. In the below sample program, we'll use the book management API from previous responses.

Launch Postman

Open the Postman application on your computer.

Create New Collection

Click the "New" button in the top left corner and select "Collection." Name it "Book Management API" and click "Create." Collections help organize your API requests.

Create Requests for Each Endpoint

Get all books (GET /books):
1. Click the "+" button next to the "Book Management API" collection to create a new request.
2. Set the HTTP method to "GET."
3. Enter the endpoint URL: http://127.0.0.1:5000/books
4. Click "Save" and name the request "Get All Books."

Get a book by ID (GET /books/:id):
1. Create a new request as before.
2. Set the HTTP method to "GET."
3. Enter the endpoint URL with a valid book ID, e.g., http://127.0.0.1:5000/books/1
4. Click "Save" and name the request "Get Book by ID."

Add a new book (POST /books):
1. Create a new request.
2. Set the HTTP method to "POST."
3. Enter the endpoint URL: http://127.0.0.1:5000/books
4. Go to the "Body" tab, select "raw" and set the format to "JSON."
5. Enter a JSON object representing the new book, e.g.,

```json
{

    "title": "Book Four",

    "author": "Author Four"

}
```

6. Click "Save" and name the request "Add New Book."

Update a book (PUT /books/:id):
1. Create a new request.
2. Set the HTTP method to "PUT."
3. Enter the endpoint URL with a valid book ID, e.g., http://127.0.0.1:5000/books/1
4. Go to the "Body" tab, select "raw" and set the format to "JSON."
5. Enter a JSON object with the updated book information, e.g.,

```json
{

    "title": "Updated Book Title",
```

```
    "author": "Updated Author"
}
```

6. Click "Save" and name the request "Update Book."

Delete a book (DELETE /books/:id):
1. Create a new request.
2. Set the HTTP method to "DELETE."
3. Enter the endpoint URL with a valid book ID, e.g., http://127.0.0.1:5000/books/1
4. Click "Save" and name the request "Delete Book."

Test each request:
1. Select a request from the "Book Management API" collection.
2. Click "Send" to send the request to your API.
3. Examine the response in Postman's "Response" section. Verify that the status code, headers, and body match the expected behavior for each endpoint.
4. Repeat this process for each request in the collection.

By following these steps, you can test each endpoint of your API using Postman. This process helps ensure that your API behaves as expected, allowing you to identify and fix any issues before deploying your API to a production environment.

CHAPTER 4: API TESTING

Types of API Testing

API (Application Programming Interface) testing is the process of verifying the functionality, reliability, performance, and security of an API. APIs enable communication between different software systems, and effective testing ensures that they function correctly and meet the intended requirements. The main goal of API testing is to identify issues or discrepancies in the API's behavior, so they can be fixed before deployment.

Functional Testing

Functional testing verifies that the API performs as expected, returning correct responses based on the input parameters. This involves testing the API's endpoints, request methods, response codes, and data validation. Test cases should cover positive (expected behavior) and negative (error conditions) scenarios.

Performance Testing

Performance testing assesses the API's speed, responsiveness, and stability under various workloads. This type of testing helps determine the API's performance bottlenecks, maximum capacity, and scalability. It often involves stress, load, spike, and endurance testing to evaluate the API's behavior under different conditions.

Security Testing

Security testing ensures that the API is protected from unauthorized access, data breaches, and other security vulnerabilities. This involves testing authentication, authorization, encryption, and input validation mechanisms. Security testing also includes penetration testing to identify potential vulnerabilities that could be exploited by attackers.

Reliability Testing

Reliability testing evaluates the API's ability to consistently provide accurate and expected results over time. This involves monitoring the API's performance, error rates, and recovery from failures. Reliability testing can help identify issues with the API's infrastructure, such as network latency or server downtime.

Compatibility Testing

Compatibility testing verifies that the API works as expected across different environments, platforms, and configurations. This includes testing the API on various operating systems, browsers, and devices, as well as ensuring backward compatibility with older API versions or clients.

Documentation Testing

Documentation testing ensures that the API's documentation is accurate, comprehensive, and up-to-date. This involves reviewing the API's descriptions, examples, and usage guidelines to verify that they align with the API's actual behavior. Good documentation helps developers understand and use the API more effectively.

Different APIs Tested using Postman

Postman is a versatile tool that supports testing various API formats:

REST (Representational State Transfer)

REST is an architectural style that defines a set of constraints for creating web services. RESTful APIs use standard HTTP methods (GET, POST, PUT, DELETE) and are typically based on JSON or XML data formats. Postman offers extensive support for testing RESTful APIs, including managing headers, parameters, and authorization.

SOAP (Simple Object Access Protocol)

SOAP is a protocol for exchanging structured information in the implementation of web services. SOAP APIs use XML for message formatting and typically rely on HTTP or SMTP for transport. Postman can test SOAP APIs by sending HTTP requests with custom headers and XML payloads.

GraphQL

GraphQL is a query language for APIs that allows clients to request only the data they need, making it more efficient than traditional REST or SOAP APIs. GraphQL APIs use a single endpoint and require clients to specify the data structure they want to receive. Postman supports GraphQL testing by allowing users to create queries and mutations, manage variables, and validate responses.

gRPC (gRPC Remote Procedure Calls)

gRPC is a modern, high-performance, open-source framework for remote procedure calls (RPCs). gRPC uses HTTP/2 for transport and Protocol Buffers for efficient serialization. Although Postman does not natively support gRPC testing, there are third-party plugins like gRPC-Web or Postman-to-gRPC that enable gRPC testing within Postman.

WebSockets

WebSockets is a communication protocol that enables bidirectional, real-time communication between clients and servers over a single, long-lived connection. It is designed for use in web browsers and web servers but can be used by any client or server application. Postman recently introduced support for WebSocket APIs, allowing users to test WebSocket connections, send messages, and analyze the response.

Postman's Testing Capabilities

In addition to Request Builder, Collections and Environments, Postman offer several far better capabilities to perform API testing. They are as below:

Test Scripts

Postman supports writing test scripts using JavaScript, allowing users to create custom assertions and validate API responses. Test scripts enable automation of functional, performance, and security testing, making it easier to catch issues early in the development process and ensuring the API behaves as expected.

Example:
After sending a GET request to retrieve a user, you can write a test script to verify that the response code is 200 and the returned user object contains the expected properties:

```
pm.test("Status code is 200", function () {
    pm.response.to.have.status(200);
});


pm.test("User object has required properties", function () {
    const user = pm.response.json();
    pm.expect(user).to.have.property('id');
    pm.expect(user).to.have.property('name');
    pm.expect(user).to.have.property('email');
});
```

Runner

Postman Runner allows users to execute a series of API requests in a specified order, either within a collection or across multiple collections. The Runner feature is useful for running end-to-end tests, load tests, or simulating user flows, helping to ensure the API behaves correctly in real-world scenarios.

Example: You can use the Runner to execute a user management API collection that simulates a user sign-up flow: creating a user, retrieving the user's information, updating the user's profile, and then deleting the user account. The Runner will execute the requests in sequence and display the test results for each step.

Mock Servers

Postman allows users to create mock servers to simulate API responses without implementing the actual backend. Mock servers help facilitate parallel development, testing, and documentation efforts, allowing frontend developers to work with the API before the backend is complete.

Example: You can create a mock server for a user management API, defining expected responses for creating, retrieving, updating, and deleting users. Frontend developers can then use the mock server to build and test their application, while backend developers work on implementing the actual API.

Monitoring

Postman offers API monitoring features that allow users to schedule and automate API tests to run at specific intervals. Monitoring helps ensure that your APIs remain reliable, performant, and secure over time, as it continuously checks for issues, downtimes, or performance degradation.

Example: You can set up monitoring for your user management API, scheduling the test suite to run every hour. This helps ensure that any potential issues are caught and resolved quickly, minimizing the impact on end-users.

Integrations

Postman integrates with various third-party services and tools, including CI/CD pipelines, API management platforms, and collaboration tools. Integrations make it easy to incorporate Postman into your existing workflows and processes, streamlining development, testing, and deployment.

Example: You can integrate Postman with a CI/CD pipeline, such as Jenkins or GitLab CI, to automatically run your API test suite whenever new code is pushed to the repository.

This helps catch issues early and ensures that your APIs are tested thoroughly before being deployed to production.

To sum it up, Postman offers a comprehensive suite of testing capabilities that enable developers to create, test, and validate APIs effectively. By leveraging these features, development teams can ensure that their APIs are robust, reliable, and secure, leading to better overall system stability and user experience.

Test REST API using Python

Postman primarily supports JavaScript for writing and executing test scripts. While it's not possible to write Python code directly within Postman, you can use Python to test APIs outside of Postman using popular libraries such as requests and unittest.

The given below is an example of how to test a RESTful API using Python:

Install the requests library, if you haven't already, by running the following command:

```
pip install requests
```

Create a new Python file, e.g., api_tests.py, and import the required libraries:

```
import unittest
import requests
```

Define a class that inherits from unittest.TestCase and write test methods for each API endpoint you want to test:

```
class TestAPI(unittest.TestCase):

    BASE_URL = 'https://api.example.com'

    def test_get_users(self):
        response = requests.get(f'{self.BASE_URL}/users')
        self.assertEqual(response.status_code, 200)
        users = response.json()
```

```python
        self.assertIsInstance(users, list)
        for user in users:
            self.assertIn('id', user)
            self.assertIn('name', user)
            self.assertIn('email', user)

    def test_create_user(self):
        payload = {
            'name': 'John Doe',
            'email': 'john.doe@example.com'
        }
        response = requests.post(f'{self.BASE_URL}/users', json=payload)
        self.assertEqual(response.status_code, 201)
        user = response.json()
        self.assertEqual(user['name'], payload['name'])
        self.assertEqual(user['email'], payload['email'])

    # Add more test methods for other API endpoints...
```

Add a main() function at the end of the file to run the test suite:

python
Copy code

```python
if __name__ == '__main__':
    unittest.main()
```

Execute the test suite by running the Python file:

python api_tests.py

While this example focuses on testing a RESTful API, you can use a similar approach to test other API formats, such as SOAP, GraphQL, or gRPC. For SOAP, you may use libraries like Zeep. For GraphQL, you can use gql or graphene. For gRPC, you can use the grpcio library.

Keep in mind that since Postman doesn't support writing and executing Python code natively, you will have to run these tests outside of Postman. However, you can still use Postman for API exploration and testing with JavaScript, and then implement the corresponding tests in Python using the approach described as above.

Handle API Testing Scenarios

Ensuring that API responses match predefined schema is crucial in API testing to maintain consistency and compliance with the API specifications. Among the different schema formats available, JSON and XML are the most popular ones. This section will explain how to handle API testing scenarios concerning validation of JSON and XML schemas.

XML Schema Validation

To validate an XML response, you can use the lxml library in Python, which provides an XML Schema Definition (XSD) validator. Following is an example of how to validate an XML response against an XSD schema:

Install the lxml library, if you haven't already, by running the following command:

pip install lxml

Define an XSD schema for the XML response, e.g. response.xsd:

```
<xs:schema xmlns:xs="http://www.w3.org/2001/XMLSchema">
  <xs:element name="user">
   <xs:complexType>
    <xs:sequence>
     <xs:element name="id" type="xs:integer"/>
     <xs:element name="name" type="xs:string"/>
     <xs:element name="email" type="xs:string"/>
    </xs:sequence>
   </xs:complexType>
  </xs:element>
</xs:schema>
```

Define a test method in your Python test suite that validates the XML response against the

XSD schema:

```python
import unittest
from lxml import etree
import requests

class TestAPI(unittest.TestCase):
    BASE_URL = 'https://api.example.com'

    def test_get_user(self):
        response = requests.get(f'{self.BASE_URL}/user')
        self.assertEqual(response.status_code, 200)
        user = response.text

        # Parse the response XML and validate against the XSD schema
        schema = etree.XMLSchema(file='response.xsd')
        parser = etree.XMLParser(schema=schema)
        root = etree.fromstring(user, parser)
```

Run the test suite and ensure that the XML response passes the schema validation.

JSON Schema Validation

To validate a JSON response, you can use the jsonschema library in Python, which provides a JSON Schema validator. Following is an example of how to validate a JSON response against a JSON Schema:

Install the jsonschema library, if you haven't already, by running the following command:

```
pip install jsonschema
```

Define a JSON Schema for the JSON response, e.g. response.jsonschema:

```json
{
  "type": "object",
```

```json
  "properties": {
    "id": {"type": "integer"},
    "name": {"type": "string"},
    "email": {"type": "string"}
  },
  "required": ["id", "name", "email"]
}
```

Define a test method in your Python test suite that validates the JSON response against the JSON Schema:

```python
import unittest
import jsonschema
import requests

class TestAPI(unittest.TestCase):
    BASE_URL = 'https://api.example.com'

    def test_get_user(self):
        response = requests.get(f'{self.BASE_URL}/user')
        self.assertEqual(response.status_code, 200)
        user = response.json()

        # Validate the response JSON against the JSON schema
        with open('response.jsonschema') as f:
            schema = json.load(f)
        jsonschema.validate(user, schema)
```

Run the test suite and ensure that the JSON response passes the schema validation.

By validating API responses against predefined XML and JSON schemas, you can ensure that the API responses adhere to the expected structure and format.

Verify Parsing the Response Data

Verifying the correct parsing of response data is crucial in API testing to ensure that the API responses are accurately processed by the client application. It is vital to validate that the response data is formatted correctly and that the application can handle any errors or exceptions that may occur during parsing. The following illustration will discuss strategies for handling API testing scenarios that involve verifying the parsing of response data.

Install the requests library, if you haven't already, by running the following command:

```
pip install requests
```

Define a test method in your Python test suite that sends a GET request to the API endpoint and parses the response data:

```python
import unittest
import requests

class TestAPI(unittest.TestCase):
    BASE_URL = 'https://api.example.com'

    def test_get_user(self):
        response = requests.get(f'{self.BASE_URL}/user')
        self.assertEqual(response.status_code, 200)

        # Parse the response data and ensure that it is properly formatted
        user = response.json()
        self.assertIsInstance(user, dict)
        self.assertIn('id', user)
        self.assertIsInstance(user['id'], int)
        self.assertIn('name', user)
        self.assertIsInstance(user['name'], str)
        self.assertIn('email', user)
        self.assertIsInstance(user['email'], str)
```

Run the test suite and ensure that the response data is properly parsed.

By verifying the parsing of response data, you can ensure that the client application can properly handle the API responses and that any issues with data formatting or parsing are caught early in the development process.

Valid Response Headers

Validating the response headers is crucial in API testing to ensure adherence to API specifications and client requirements. In this subtopic, we will explore how to handle scenarios in API testing to verify response headers.

Install the requests library, if you haven't already, by running the following command:

pip install requests

Define a test method in your Python test suite that sends a GET request to the API endpoint and checks the response headers:

```python
import unittest
import requests

class TestAPI(unittest.TestCase):
    BASE_URL = 'https://api.example.com'

    def test_get_user(self):
        response = requests.get(f'{self.BASE_URL}/user')
        self.assertEqual(response.status_code, 200)

        # Check the response headers and ensure that they are correct
        self.assertIn('content-type', response.headers)
        self.assertEqual(response.headers['content-type'], 'application/json')
        self.assertIn('cache-control', response.headers)
        self.assertEqual(response.headers['cache-control'], 'max-age=3600')
        self.assertIn('x-rate-limit', response.headers)
```

```python
self.assertIsInstance(response.headers['x-rate-limit'], str)
```

Run the test suite and ensure that the response headers are correct.

By verifying the response headers, you can ensure that the API responses adhere to the specification and meet the client's requirements.

Negative Testcase Response

To ensure that an API can handle errors and exceptions that may occur during usage, it's crucial to perform negative testing. Negative testing involves testing scenarios where unexpected inputs or conditions are encountered. In this way, developers can ensure that their API is robust and can handle any issues that may arise in the real world. This particular topic teaches how to handle negative testing scenarios in API testing.

Install the requests library, if you haven't already, by running the following command:

```
pip install requests
```

Define a test method in your Python test suite that sends a request to the API endpoint with invalid parameters and checks the response status code and message:

```python
import unittest
import requests

class TestAPI(unittest.TestCase):
    BASE_URL = 'https://api.example.com'

    def test_invalid_user_id(self):
        response = requests.get(f'{self.BASE_URL}/user?id=abc')
        self.assertEqual(response.status_code, 400)
        error = response.json()
        self.assertIsInstance(error, dict)
        self.assertIn('message', error)
        self.assertEqual(error['message'], 'Invalid user ID')
```

Run the test suite and ensure that the API can properly handle invalid parameters and returns the correct error response.

Testing negative test cases is important as it helps to ensure that the API can handle errors or exceptions that may occur during usage and provide the necessary feedback to the client application. This can contribute to the overall improvement of the API's reliability and user experience.

Verify the Response HTTP Status Code

One of the another essential aspects is to verify that the API responses include the correct HTTP status codes. This ensures that the APIs comply with the API specification and meet the client's needs.

The below example will explain how to handle various API testing scenarios and how to verify the response HTTP status code, which is an essential step in API testing.

Install the requests library, if you haven't already, by running the following command:

```
pip install requests
```

Define a test method in your Python test suite that sends a request to the API endpoint and checks the response status code:

```python
import unittest
import requests

class TestAPI(unittest.TestCase):
    BASE_URL = 'https://api.example.com'

    def test_get_user(self):
        response = requests.get(f'{self.BASE_URL}/user')
        self.assertEqual(response.status_code, 200)
```

Run the test suite and ensure that the response HTTP status code is correct.

By verifying the response HTTP status code, you can ensure that the API responses adhere to the specification and meet the client's requirements. This can help improve the overall reliability and performance of the API.

Verify Valid Response Payload

Validating API responses to ensure that they comply with API specifications and fulfill client requirements is critical in API testing. This involves verifying that the payload data in the API responses is accurate. In the below given sample illustration, we will cover how to handle API testing scenarios on verifying the response payload data.

Install the requests library, if you haven't already, by running the following command:

```
pip install requests
```

Define a test method in your Python test suite that sends a GET request to the API endpoint and checks the response payload:

```python
import unittest
import requests

class TestAPI(unittest.TestCase):
    BASE_URL = 'https://api.example.com'

    def test_get_user(self):
        response = requests.get(f'{self.BASE_URL}/user')
        self.assertEqual(response.status_code, 200)

        # Check the response payload and ensure that it is correct
        user = response.json()
        self.assertIsInstance(user, dict)
        self.assertIn('id', user)
        self.assertIsInstance(user['id'], int)
        self.assertIn('name', user)
        self.assertIsInstance(user['name'], str)
        self.assertIn('email', user)
```

```python
        self.assertIsInstance(user['email'], str)
```

Run the test suite and ensure that the response payload is correct.

By verifying the response payload, you can ensure that the API responses adhere to the specification and meet the client's requirements. This can help improve the overall reliability and performance of the API.

End-to-end CRUD Flows

To ensure proper functionality of an API, testing the complete end-to-end CRUD (Create, Read, Update, Delete) flow is crucial in API testing. It is essential to verify that the API can handle all operations as intended. In the below given sample illustration, we will cover how to handle API testing scenarios on end-to-end CRUD flows.

Install the requests library, if you haven't already, by running the following command:

```
pip install requests
```

Define a test method in your Python test suite that performs the end-to-end CRUD flow:

```python
import unittest
import requests

class TestAPI(unittest.TestCase):
    BASE_URL = 'https://api.example.com'

    def test_crud_flow(self):
        # Create a new user
        data = {'name': 'John Doe', 'email': 'johndoe@example.com'}
        response = requests.post(f'{self.BASE_URL}/user', json=data)
        self.assertEqual(response.status_code, 201)
        user_id = response.json()['id']

        # Read the user data
        response = requests.get(f'{self.BASE_URL}/user/{user_id}')
```

```python
        self.assertEqual(response.status_code, 200)
        user = response.json()
        self.assertIsInstance(user, dict)
        self.assertIn('id', user)
        self.assertEqual(user['id'], user_id)
        self.assertIn('name', user)
        self.assertIsInstance(user['name'], str)
        self.assertEqual(user['name'], data['name'])
        self.assertIn('email', user)
        self.assertIsInstance(user['email'], str)
        self.assertEqual(user['email'], data['email'])

        # Update the user data
        new_data = {'name': 'Jane Doe', 'email': 'janedoe@example.com'}
        response = requests.put(f'{self.BASE_URL}/user/{user_id}',
json=new_data)
        self.assertEqual(response.status_code, 200)
        updated_user = response.json()
        self.assertIsInstance(updated_user, dict)
        self.assertIn('id', updated_user)
        self.assertEqual(updated_user['id'], user_id)
        self.assertIn('name', updated_user)
        self.assertIsInstance(updated_user['name'], str)
        self.assertEqual(updated_user['name'], new_data['name'])
        self.assertIn('email', updated_user)
        self.assertIsInstance(updated_user['email'], str)
        self.assertEqual(updated_user['email'], new_data['email'])

        # Delete the user
        response = requests.delete(f'{self.BASE_URL}/user/{user_id}')
        self.assertEqual(response.status_code, 204)
```

```python
# Attempt to read the deleted user data (should return 404)
response = requests.get(f'{self.BASE_URL}/user/{user_id}')
self.assertEqual(response.status_code, 404)
```

Run the test suite and ensure that the end-to-end CRUD flow is successful and all operations are properly handled.

By testing the full end-to-end CRUD flow, you can ensure that the API can properly handle all operations and functions as expected, and that any issues or bugs are caught early in the development process. This can help improve the overall reliability and functionality of the API.

Chapter 5: API Security

API Threats Landscape

API (Application Programming Interface) security threats refer to potential risks and vulnerabilities that can compromise the confidentiality, integrity, and availability of API systems and the data they process. APIs are essential for interconnecting software applications and services, but they can also expose sensitive information and create entry points for malicious attacks.

Following are some common API security threats conceptually:

Injection attacks

Attackers send malicious data to an API, which is then executed or processed, leading to unauthorized access, data theft, or other adverse effects. Common examples include SQL injection, command injection, and code injection attacks.

Authentication and authorization flaws

Weak or improperly implemented authentication and authorization mechanisms can allow unauthorized users to gain access to sensitive data or perform unauthorized actions. Examples include insufficient authentication, weak passwords, and broken access controls.

Insecure communication

Unencrypted or weakly encrypted communication between clients and APIs can be intercepted, eavesdropped, or tampered with by attackers. This can lead to sensitive data exposure, man-in-the-middle attacks, or other attacks compromising data integrity and confidentiality.

Sensitive data exposure

APIs can inadvertently expose sensitive data, such as personal or financial information, if they are not designed and configured with proper security controls. This can result from issues like insufficient data encryption or insecure data storage.

Parameter tampering

Attackers may manipulate API parameters, such as URL or request parameters, to bypass security controls or gain unauthorized access to data and resources.

XML External Entity (XXE) attacks

APIs that process XML input can be vulnerable to XXE attacks, where attackers exploit external entity references to access sensitive data, perform server-side request forgery (SSRF), or execute arbitrary code.

Denial of Service (DoS) attacks

Attackers can overwhelm an API by sending a high volume of requests, consuming its resources, and rendering it unable to process legitimate requests. This can lead to service disruptions and performance degradation.

Insufficient logging and monitoring

Inadequate logging and monitoring can make it difficult to detect security incidents and respond to attacks, allowing attackers to exploit vulnerabilities and access sensitive data undetected.

Misconfigurations

Poorly configured APIs can expose sensitive information, leave security vulnerabilities unaddressed, or allow unauthorized access. Examples include default credentials, unpatched software, or insecure deployment configurations.

Insecure API design and implementation

Design flaws in APIs, such as improper input validation, error handling, or data processing, can lead to security vulnerabilities that can be exploited by attackers.

To mitigate these threats, organizations should adopt best practices for API security, such as following the OWASP API Security Top 10 and implementing robust security controls throughout the API lifecycle.

Prevent Injection Attacks

Postman is a popular tool for testing and developing APIs but it's also important to note that Postman itself is not responsible for preventing injection attacks like SQL, command, or code injection. These attacks must be mitigated at the API implementation level, in your server-side code.

That being said, we can provide you with some general guidelines on how to prevent these types of attacks in your API implementation:

SQL Injection

To prevent SQL injection attacks, you should use parameterized queries, prepared statements, or stored procedures instead of concatenating user input directly into SQL queries. Following is an example using prepared statements in Node.js with the MySQL library:

```javascript
const mysql = require('mysql');
const connection = mysql.createConnection({
  host: 'localhost',
  user: 'your_user',
  password: 'your_password',
  database: 'your_database'
});


connection.connect();


// Get user input from the API request
const userInput = req.body.userInput;


// Use a prepared statement to prevent SQL injection
const query = 'SELECT * FROM your_table WHERE column_name = ?';
connection.query(query, [userInput], (error, results, fields) => {
  if (error) {
    console.error('An error occurred: ' + error.message);
    return;
  }


  console.log('Query results:', results);
});


connection.end();
```

Command Injection

To prevent command injection attacks, you should avoid using user input directly in shell commands. If you must use user input, you should validate and sanitize it, and use proper escaping mechanisms provided by your programming language. Following is an example using Node.js to execute a command safely:

```javascript
const { execFile } = require('child_process');

// Get user input from the API request
const userInput = req.body.userInput;

// Validate and sanitize user input before using it in a command
if (isValid(userInput)) {
  const sanitizedInput = sanitize(userInput);

  // Use execFile instead of exec to avoid command injection
  execFile('your_command', [sanitizedInput], (error, stdout, stderr) => {
    if (error) {
      console.error('An error occurred: ' + error.message);
      return;
    }

    console.log('Command output:', stdout);
  });
} else {
  console.error('Invalid user input');
}
```

Code Injection

To prevent code injection attacks, you should never execute user input as code. You should also validate and sanitize user input before using it in any logic or data manipulation. For example, when using JavaScript's eval() function or other dynamic code execution methods, you should avoid passing any user input directly:

```javascript
// Get user input from the API request
const userInput = req.body.userInput;

// Validate and sanitize user input before using it in any logic or data
```

```javascript
manipulation
if (isValid(userInput)) {
  const sanitizedInput = sanitize(userInput);

  // Avoid using eval() or other dynamic code execution methods with user input
  const result = someSafeFunction(sanitizedInput);

  console.log('Result:', result);
} else {
  console.error('Invalid user input');
}
```

The above ones are few of my practices on how to prevent injection attacks in your API implementation.

Prevent Authentication & Authorization Flaws

To prevent insufficient authentication, weak passwords, and broken access controls, you should implement robust security measures in your API. I'll provide you with a practical example using Node.js, Express, and the Passport library for authentication. We'll also use bcrypt for password hashing and JWT for access control.

Install the required packages

```
npm install express passport passport-jwt passport-local bcrypt jsonwebtoken
```

Create a basic Express app and include the necessary libraries:

```javascript
const express = require('express');
const passport = require('passport');
const LocalStrategy = require('passport-local').Strategy;
const JwtStrategy = require('passport-jwt').Strategy;
const ExtractJwt = require('passport-jwt').ExtractJwt;
```

```javascript
const bcrypt = require('bcrypt');
const jwt = require('jsonwebtoken');

const app = express();
app.use(express.json());
```

Implement user storage and password hashing (replace this with your actual database):

```javascript
// Example user storage (use your actual database in production)
const users = [
  {
    id: 1,
    username: 'user1',
    password:
'$2b$10$DxkGJbY7K8cXzgV7bEoAAeKp7.P8c1ZwVVEeLrjQr3YkjzIZn3e9
e' // bcrypt hashed password for "password1"
  }
];

// Function to hash a plaintext password
async function hashPassword(password) {
  const saltRounds = 10;
  return await bcrypt.hash(password, saltRounds);
}

// Function to verify a plaintext password against a hashed password
async function verifyPassword(password, hashedPassword) {
  return await bcrypt.compare(password, hashedPassword);
}
```

Set up Passport local strategy for user authentication:

```
passport.use(new LocalStrategy(async (username, password, done) => {
  const user = users.find(user => user.username === username);

  if (!user) {
    return done(null, false, { message: 'Incorrect username.' });
  }

  const isValidPassword = await verifyPassword(password, user.password);
  if (!isValidPassword) {
    return done(null, false, { message: 'Incorrect password.' });
  }

  return done(null, user);
}));
```

Set up Passport JWT strategy for access control:

```
const jwtOptions = {
  jwtFromRequest: ExtractJwt.fromAuthHeaderAsBearerToken(),
  secretOrKey: 'your_jwt_secret'
};

passport.use(new JwtStrategy(jwtOptions, (jwtPayload, done) => {
  const user = users.find(user => user.id === jwtPayload.id);

  if (user) {
    return done(null, user);
  } else {
    return done(null, false);
  }
}
```

}));

Implement login route with proper authentication:

```
app.post('/login', (req, res, next) => {
  passport.authenticate('local', { session: false }, (err, user, info) => {
    if (err || !user) {
      return res.status(400).json({ message: 'Login failed', user: user });
    }

    req.login(user, { session: false }, (err) => {
      if (err) {
        return res.status(400).send(err);
      }

    const token = jwt.sign({ id: user.id }, jwtOptions.secretOrKey, { expiresIn:
'1h' });
      return res.json({ user, token });
    });
  })(req, res);
});
```

Protect routes with JWT authentication:

```
app.get('/protected', passport.authenticate('jwt', { session: false }), (req, res,
next) => {
res.json({ message: 'This is a protected route', user: req.user });
});
```

Start the server:

```
const port = process.env.PORT || 3000;
```

```
app.listen(port, () => {
  console.log(`Server running on port ${port}`);
});
```

Now, you have a Node.js API that demonstrates proper authentication using Passport's local strategy, password hashing using bcrypt, and access control using JWT tokens. Users can log in with their credentials, receive a JWT token, and use that token to access protected routes. This demontration should be adapted to your specific use case, and you should replace the example user storage with your actual database, without fail.

Remember, this is just one example using Node.js, Express, and Passport but the principles remain the same across different programming languages and frameworks, i.e., implement strong authentication, use password hashing for storing passwords, and enforce access control using tokens or other mechanisms. Always follow best practices for secure coding in your specific language and framework.

Protect from MITM Attacks

The key to preventing man-in-the-middle (MITM) attacks is to secure the communication between the client and the server. Postman is an API testing and development tool that doesn't directly prevent MITM attacks, but it can be leveraged to ensure secure communication when sending requests to your API. With Postman, you can specify the protocol (HTTP or HTTPS), the request headers, and the request body, all of which can help secure your communication. Postman also supports setting up and using client-side SSL certificates, which can provide an extra layer of security. While Postman is not a comprehensive security tool, it can be a useful component of a broader security strategy for your API.

The given below procedure is how you can configure Postman to send requests securely:

Use HTTPS for API Endpoints

When setting up your API, make sure to use HTTPS instead of HTTP. HTTPS encrypts the communication between the client and the server, making it difficult for an attacker to intercept, read, or modify the data being transmitted.

In Postman, when sending requests to your API, use the HTTPS protocol in your URL:

https://your-api.example.com/your-endpoint

<u>Verify SSL/TLS Certificates</u>

By default, Postman will verify SSL/TLS certificates to ensure that the server you are communicating with is the legitimate server and not an imposter. This helps prevent MITM attacks where an attacker poses as the server to intercept or modify data.

To ensure that Postman verifies SSL/TLS certificates, go to the Postman settings:
- Click on the gear icon in the top-right corner to open the Settings modal.
- In the "General" tab, make sure that the "SSL certificate verification" option is enabled (toggle set to "ON").
- Use client certificates if necessary:

In some cases, you might need to use client certificates for additional security. Client certificates are used to authenticate the client to the server, ensuring that the server only accepts connections from trusted clients. This can help prevent MITM attacks by ensuring that the server only communicates with authorized clients.

To configure client certificates in Postman:
- Click on the gear icon in the top-right corner to open the Settings modal.
- Go to the "Certificates" tab.
- Click on "Add Certificate."
- Enter the hostname for your API and upload the certificate (CRT) and private key (KEY) files. Optionally, you can also upload a CA (Certificate Authority) file.

Remember, preventing MITM attacks involves more than just configuring Postman. You should also configure your server to enforce strong SSL/TLS settings and keep your server's software up-to-date with security patches. Additionally, ensure your API users are aware of security best practices, such as not clicking on suspicious links or downloading untrusted software that could facilitate MITM attacks.

Safeguard Parameter Tampering

Parameter tampering is a type of cyber attack where a hacker manipulates URL or request parameters to exploit vulnerabilities in a system, gain access to sensitive data, or bypass security controls. To protect against parameter tampering, it is important to implement input validation, use parameterized queries, and avoid revealing sensitive information in URL parameters. Input validation ensures that user input is valid and meets specific requirements, while parameterized queries protect against SQL injection attacks. Avoiding sensitive information in URL parameters reduces the risk of exposing data to attackers. By implementing these measures, organizations can better protect their systems and data from parameter tampering attacks.

The given below is an example of how to prevent parameter tampering in an API implemented with Node.js and Express:

Install express-validator package for input validation:

```
npm install express-validator
```

Create a basic Express app and include the necessary libraries:

```
const express = require('express');
const { body, validationResult } = require('express-validator');

const app = express();
app.use(express.json());
```

Implement a route that receives user input from the request parameters and apply input validation:

```
app.post('/submit', [
  // Validate user input
  body('userId').isInt().toInt(),
  body('email').isEmail().normalizeEmail(),
  body('comment').trim().isLength({ min: 1, max: 500 })
], (req, res) => {
  // Check for validation errors
  const errors = validationResult(req);
  if (!errors.isEmpty()) {
    return res.status(400).json({ errors: errors.array() });
  }

  // Process the request safely with validated parameters
  const { userId, email, comment } = req.body;
  console.log(`User ID: ${userId}, Email: ${email}, Comment: ${comment}`);
```

```
  res.json({ message: 'Request processed successfully', data: { userId, email,
comment } });
});
```

In the above sample program, the express-validator middleware is used to validate and sanitize the input parameters before they are processed by the route. This helps prevent parameter tampering by ensuring that only valid and properly formatted input is accepted.

Remember that this is just one of my experience of using Node.js and Express. The principles of input validation and secure handling of request parameters apply across different programming languages and frameworks and as said previously, do not forget to implement proper input validation and adhere to best practices for secure coding in your selected language and respective framework.

Prevent XXE Attacks

XML External Entity (XXE) attacks exploit vulnerabilities in XML parsers by including malicious external entity references in XML documents, resulting in unauthorized data access or denial of service attacks. To prevent XXE attacks, it is crucial to configure XML parsers to disable external entities and implement secure handling of XML input. This can be achieved by using secure coding practices and implementing input validation to ensure that only trusted sources can provide XML input. By taking these precautions, developers can mitigate the risk of XXE attacks and improve the security of their applications.

The given below is an example of how to prevent XXE attacks in a Node.js application using the libxmljs library for XML parsing:

Install the libxmljs package:

```
npm install libxmljs
```

Create a basic Express app and include the necessary libraries:

```
const express = require('express');
const libxmljs = require('libxmljs');
```

```javascript
const app = express();
app.use(express.text({ type: 'application/xml' }));
```

Implement a route that receives an XML document in the request body and configure the XML parser to disable external entities:

```javascript
app.post('/process-xml', (req, res) => {
  // Get the XML input from the request body
  const xmlInput = req.body;

  // Check if the request contains XML data
  if (!xmlInput || typeof xmlInput !== 'string') {
    return res.status(400).json({ message: 'Invalid XML data' });
  }

  try {
    // Parse the XML input with external entities disabled
    const xmlDoc = libxmljs.parseXmlString(xmlInput, { noent: false, dtdload:
false });

    // Process the parsed XML document safely
    const result = processXmlSafely(xmlDoc);
    res.json({ message: 'XML processed successfully', data: result });
  } catch (error) {
    console.error('An error occurred while processing the XML:', error.message);
    res.status(500).json({ message: 'Failed to process the XML' });
  }
});

function processXmlSafely(xmlDoc) {
  // Implement your XML processing logic here, using the parsed xmlDoc
  // ...
```

```
return {}; // Return the result of your processing
}
```

In the above sample program, the libxmljs library is used to parse the XML input with the noent and dtdload options set to false. This disables the processing of external entities, effectively preventing XXE attacks.

Prevent DDoS Attacks

Mitigating Distributed Denial of Service (DDoS) attacks involves implementing measures on the server-side infrastructure to detect and block malicious traffic. While Postman cannot directly prevent DDoS attacks, it can be utilized to test server-side protections such as rate-limiting. By running a Postman Collection that simulates high traffic requests to your API, you can test whether your rate-limiting and other server-side protections are functioning as intended to mitigate DDoS attacks. Postman's testing capabilities enable developers to proactively test and identify vulnerabilities in their server-side infrastructure before an actual attack occurs. By regularly testing and improving your server-side protections, you can minimize the impact of DDoS attacks on your API's performance and uptime, ensuring that your users have uninterrupted access to your services.

For this example, I'll show you how to implement rate-limiting in a Node.js application using Express and the express-rate-limit package. You can then use Postman to test the rate-limiting functionality.

Install the express-rate-limit package:

npm install express-rate-limit

Create a basic Express app and include the necessary libraries:

```
const express = require('express');
const rateLimit = require('express-rate-limit');


const app = express();
```

Implement rate-limiting middleware:

```
const limiter = rateLimit({
  windowMs: 1 * 60 * 1000, // 1 minute
  max: 5, // Limit each IP to 5 requests per windowMs
  message: "Too many requests, please try again later."
});


// Apply the rate-limiting middleware to all routes
app.use(limiter);
```

Implement a simple route for testing:

```
app.get('/test', (req, res) => {
  res.json({ message: 'This route is rate-limited' });
});
```

Start the server:

```
const port = process.env.PORT || 3000;
app.listen(port, () => {
  console.log(`Server running on port ${port}`);
});
```

Now that you have a rate-limited API, you can use Postman to test the rate-limiting functionality:
- Open Postman.
- Create a new GET request to your API endpoint, for example:

http://localhost:3000/test

Send multiple requests in a short period. After you hit the rate limit (5 requests in this example), you should receive a response with the message "Too many requests, please try again later."

Keep in mind that rate-limiting is just one of the many measures that can help protect your server against DDoS attacks. You may also need a combination of strategies, including traffic filtering, content delivery networks (CDNs), and other security best practices. Postman is a useful tool for testing these server-side protections but is not a direct solution for preventing DDoS attacks.

CHAPTER 6: USING POSTMAN CLI

Understand Postman CLI

Postman CLI is a command line tool that helps API developers automate and streamline their API testing and integration workflows. It enables users to run, manage, and monitor API requests, collections, and environments without a graphical user interface. Postman CLI offers a flexible and powerful solution for executing API tests and integrations, making it a valuable tool for API developers in their daily work. With Postman CLI, developers can quickly test and verify API functionality, integrate APIs with other systems, and automate testing and integration workflows. Postman CLI can be easily integrated with CI/CD pipelines, making it an essential tool for building and deploying reliable and high-performance APIs. By leveraging Postman CLI, developers can improve the quality, performance, and efficiency of their APIs, enabling them to deliver high-quality services to their users.

Advantages of Postman CLI

Automation

One of the main advantages of using Postman CLI is automation. With the CLI, you can automate your API testing and integration tasks and reduce the time and effort required to perform these tasks manually. You can write scripts to run your collections and tests, which can be scheduled to run at specific intervals or triggered by events such as code changes or deployments.

Customization

Postman CLI provides a high degree of customization, allowing you to tailor your API testing and integration workflows to your specific requirements. You can customize your environment variables, headers, and request bodies, and write scripts to perform custom actions based on the results of your tests. This level of customization makes Postman CLI a powerful tool for API developers who need to perform complex tasks and workflows.

Collaboration

Postman CLI also enables collaboration between team members working on the same API project. You can share your collections, tests, and environments with other team members, and they can run these from their local machines using the CLI. This helps to ensure consistency and accuracy in testing and integration, and reduces the risk of errors and inconsistencies.

Reusability

Postman CLI provides a high degree of reusability, allowing you to reuse collections, tests, and environments across different projects and workflows. You can create templates and variables that can be reused across different collections, and write scripts that can be used across different tests. This helps to reduce the time and effort required to create and maintain your API testing and integration workflows.

Scalability

Postman CLI provides scalability, allowing you to run your API tests and integrations at scale. You can run your tests and integrations across multiple environments and configurations, and scale your tests to handle large volumes of requests. This helps to ensure that your API is performing as expected under various load conditions and helps to identify and fix performance issues before they impact your users.

How Postman CLI Benefits API Developers

Faster API Testing

API testing is an essential part of API development, and Postman CLI can help API developers to perform this task more efficiently. By automating API testing, Postman CLI reduces the time and effort required to run tests manually, and provides a consistent and reliable way to test your APIs. This helps API developers to identify and fix issues quickly and ensure that their APIs are functioning as expected.

Streamlined API Integration

API integration is another critical aspect of API development, and Postman CLI can help API developers to streamline this process. By automating API integrations, Postman CLI reduces the time and effort required to integrate APIs, and provides a consistent and reliable way to integrate APIs. This helps API developers to build better integrations more quickly and efficiently.

Consistent API Testing and Integration

Postman CLI provides a consistent way to test and integrate APIs, which helps to ensure that your APIs are performing as expected across different environments and configurations. This consistency helps to reduce the risk of errors and inconsistencies, and ensures that your APIs are reliable and consistent for your users.

Better Collaboration

Postman CLI enables better collaboration between API developers, QA engineers, and other stakeholders involved in API development. By sharing collections, tests, and environments, team members can work together more effectively and ensure that everyone is on the same page when it comes to API testing and integration.

Improved API Quality and Performance

Postman CLI can help API developers to improve the quality and performance of their APIs. By automating API testing and integration, Postman CLI helps API developers to identify and fix issues quickly and efficiently, which can improve the quality of their APIs. By scaling API tests, Postman CLI helps API developers to identify and fix performance issues before they impact users, which can improve the performance of their APIs.

Reduced Development Time and Costs

Postman CLI can help API developers to reduce development time and costs by streamlining API testing and integration workflows. By automating these tasks, Postman CLI reduces the time and effort required to perform them manually, which can help API developers to develop APIs more quickly and efficiently. This, in turn, can help to reduce development costs and improve the overall efficiency of the API development process.

Increased Flexibility

Postman CLI provides API developers with a high degree of flexibility when it comes to API testing and integration. By providing a wide range of customization options and scripting capabilities, Postman CLI enables API developers to tailor their workflows to their specific requirements. This flexibility helps API developers to build better APIs more efficiently and can help to improve the overall quality of their APIs.

Installing Postman CLI

To install Postman CLI, follow the steps below:
- Step 1: Open your terminal or command prompt.
- Step 2: Check if Node.js is installed on your system by running the command node -v. If Node.js is not installed, download and install it from the official website.
- Step 3: Install Postman CLI by running the command npm install -g postman-cli. This will install the Postman CLI globally on your system.
- Step 4: Verify that Postman CLI is installed correctly by running the command postman --version. This should display the version number of Postman CLI installed on your system.
- Step 5: Since you already have Postman installed and configured, you can now import your collections and environments to Postman CLI. To do this, navigate to your Postman collection and click the Export button. Choose the format as Collection v2.1 and save the file.
- Step 6: Open your terminal and navigate to the directory where you saved the exported collection file.
- Step 7: To import the collection to Postman CLI, run the command postman import collection /path/to/collection.json. Replace /path/to/collection.json with

the actual path to your collection file.

- Step 8: You can now run your collection using Postman CLI by running the command postman run <collection_name>. Replace <collection_name> with the name of your collection.
- Step 9: To view the results of your collection run, run the command postman run <collection_name> --reporters cli,html --reporter-html-export /path/to/report.html. This will generate an HTML report of your collection run, which you can view in your web browser.

With this, you have successfully installed and configured Postman CLI and executed your first collection. There are many other features and commands provided by Postman CLI that you can explore to further enhance your API testing and integration workflows. These features and commands can help streamline your API testing process, improve the quality and performance of your APIs, and ensure that they meet the needs of your users.

Run Collection from Postman CLI

Postman Collections are a set of requests that are grouped together to form a suite of API tests. Collections can be organized into folders, and each request within a collection can have its own set of parameters, such as headers, query parameters, and request body. Collections can be imported and exported in various formats, making it easy to share collections with other team members.

To run a collection from Postman CLI, you first need to import the collection into Postman. Once you have done that, you can use the newman command-line tool, which is a part of Postman CLI, to run the collection.

The given below is a step-by-step solution on how to run a collection from Postman CLI using a sample demonstration of more than 10 collections:

Install Postman CLI

To install Postman CLI, follow the instructions provided in the previous section.

Import Sample Collection

For this demonstration, we will use a sample collection called "Postman Echo." You can download this collection from the Postman API Network by clicking on this link: https://explore.postman.com/templates/8062/postman-echo

Once you have downloaded the collection, import it into Postman by following these steps:

Open Postman and click on the "Import" button in the top left corner.

Select the "Import From Link" option.

Paste the link to the Postman Echo collection and click on the "Import" button.

Verify Collection Import

To verify that the collection has been imported successfully, click on the "Collections" tab in the left-hand navigation menu. You should see the Postman Echo collection listed there.

Install Newman

Newman is a command-line tool that is used to run Postman collections from the CLI. To install Newman, open your terminal or command prompt and run the following command:

```
npm install -g newman
```

Run the Collection

To run the Postman Echo collection using Newman, open your terminal or command prompt and navigate to the directory where the collection is located. Then, run the following command:

```
newman run "Postman Echo.postman_collection.json"
```

This will start the collection run, and you will see the results in your terminal or command prompt window. The output will look something like this:

```
Postman Echo

→ GET /get

  OK

...
```

→ POST /post

OK

...

→ PUT /put

OK

...

→ PATCH /patch

OK

...

→ DELETE /delete

OK

...

→ GET /status/200

OK

...

→ GET /status/201

OK

...

→ GET /status/400

OK

...

→ GET /status/401

OK

...

→ GET /status/403

OK

...

→ GET /status/404

OK

...

→ GET /status/500

OK

...

→ GET /stream/5

OK

...

→ GET /delay/3

OK

...

→ GET /gzip

OK

...

→ GET /deflate

OK

...

→ GET /brotli

OK

...

→ GET /cache

 OK

 ...

→ GET /response-headers?key=value

 OK

 ...

→ GET /cookies

 OK

 ...

→ GET /headers

 OK

 ...

→ GET /image/png

 OK

 ...

→ GET /xml

OK

...

→ GET /json

OK

...

→ GET /html

OK

...

→ GET /

View the Collection Results

Once the collection run is complete, you can view the results in your terminal or command prompt window. The results will show whether each request in the collection was successful or not, along with any response data or errors that were returned.

Running Multiple Collections

If you want to run multiple collections, you can do so by specifying the path to each collection file in the newman run command. For example, if you have 10 collections in a directory called "collections," you can run all of them using the following command:

```
newman run collections/*.json
```

This will run all the collections in the "collections" directory.

Setting Up GitHub Actions using Postman CLI

GitHub Actions is a powerful tool that enables developers to automate their software development workflows. With GitHub Actions, developers can build, test, and deploy their code directly from their GitHub repositories, without the need for separate CI/CD tools.

Setting up GitHub Actions with Postman CLI can be a powerful way to automate API testing and integration workflows as part of the software development process. Following is a step-by-step walkthrough on how to set up GitHub Actions with Postman CLI using a sample demonstration:

Create GitHub Repository

If you haven't already, create a new GitHub repository or select an existing repository that you want to use for your API testing and integration workflows.

Install Postman CLI

Before you can use Postman CLI with GitHub Actions, you need to install it on your local machine. Follow the instructions provided in the previous section to install Postman CLI.

Create Postman Collection

Create a new Postman Collection or use an existing one that you want to use for your API testing and integration workflows.

Create Workflow

To create a new GitHub Actions workflow, navigate to your GitHub repository and click on the "Actions" tab. Then, click on the "New workflow" button.

Choose Template

GitHub provides several workflow templates to choose from. For this demonstration, we will use the "Node.js with Postman" template. Select the template and click on the "Set up this workflow" button.

Configure the Workflow

The template will create a basic workflow file in YAML format. You can customize this file to meet your specific requirements. In this demonstration, we will use the default configuration.

Add Your Postman Collection

In the workflow file, add a step to download your Postman Collection from your repository. You can use the following code to do this:

```
- name: Download Postman Collection
  uses: actions/checkout@v2
```

Run Your Postman Collection

Next, add a step to run your Postman Collection using Newman. You can use the following code to do this:

```
- name: Run Postman Collection
  run: newman run /path/to/your/collection.json
```

Replace /path/to/your/collection.json with the actual path to your Postman Collection.

Save and Commit Your Workflow File

Once you have configured your workflow file, save it and commit it to your GitHub repository.

Test Your Workflow

To test your workflow, navigate to the "Actions" tab in your GitHub repository and click on the workflow that you just created. GitHub Actions will automatically run your workflow and display the results in the "Actions" tab.

By and after integrating GitHub Actions with Postman CLI, developers can automate their API testing and integration workflows as part of the software development process, improving the quality, performance, and efficiency of their APIs.

Run Collections inside CI/CD Pipeline

Integrating Postman Collections in CI/CD pipelines ensures that APIs are thoroughly tested and integrated before they are deployed. The process involves defining a workflow with GitHub Actions, installing Postman CLI, creating a Postman Collection, and running it using Newman. To run the collections inside a CI/CD pipeline, you can use Jenkins and schedule the pipeline to run regularly. This automates the testing and integration process and ensures the quality, performance, and reliability of your APIs.

The given below procedure is how to run Postman Collections inside a CI/CD pipeline:

Create Workflow File

Create a new workflow file in your repository. This file should be saved in the .github/workflows directory of your repository and should be named postman.yml (or any name you choose).

Define the Workflow

In the workflow file, define the steps that your CI/CD pipeline should perform. The following example demonstrates how to use GitHub Actions to run a Postman Collection using Newman:

```
name: Postman CI

on:
 push:
  branches:
   - main

jobs:
 build:
  runs-on: ubuntu-latest

  steps:
   - name: Checkout code
     uses: actions/checkout@v2

   - name: Install Newman
```

```
    run: npm install -g newman

  - name: Run Postman Collection
    run: newman run /path/to/your/collection.json
```

In the above demonstrated sample, the workflow will be triggered when code is pushed to the main branch. The build job will run on an Ubuntu environment and consists of three steps:

Checking out Code

The first step in running a Postman Collection inside a CI/CD pipeline is to check out the code from your repository. This can be done using the actions/checkout GitHub Action. Following is an example of how to check out the code:

```
- name: Checkout code
  uses: actions/checkout@v2
```

This will clone your repository to the runner machine, making it available for the following steps.

Installing Newman

The next step is to install Newman on the runner machine. This can be done using the npm command, as follows:

```
- name: Install Newman
  run: npm install -g newman
```

This will install the latest version of Newman globally on the runner machine.

Running the Postman Collection

Once Newman is installed, you can use it to run your Postman Collection. Following is an example of how to run a Postman Collection:

```
- name: Run Postman Collection
```

```
run: newman run /path/to/your/collection.json
```

Replace /path/to/your/collection.json with the actual path to your Postman Collection. This will execute the Postman Collection using Newman and output the results to the console.

Save and Commit Your Workflow File

Once you have defined your workflow file, save it and commit it to your GitHub repository.

Verify Your Workflow

To verify your workflow, navigate to the "Actions" tab in your GitHub repository and click on the workflow that you just created. GitHub Actions will automatically run your workflow and display the results in the "Actions" tab.

To sum it up, running Postman Collections inside CI/CD pipelines is an effective way to automate API testing and integration as part of the software development process. By integrating Postman CLI and Newman with your CI/CD pipeline, you can ensure that your APIs are thoroughly tested and integrated before they are deployed to production. This helps to improve the quality, performance, and reliability of your APIs, and helps to ensure that they meet the needs of your users.

Automate Postman Collections

Automating Postman collections involves running the collections on a scheduled basis, such as daily or weekly, without the need for manual intervention. This can be accomplished using various tools and services, such as Jenkins, CircleCI, or Travis CI. Following is an example of how to automate Postman collections using Jenkins:

Install Jenkins

First, install Jenkins on your server or local machine. Jenkins is a popular open-source automation server that can be used to automate various tasks, including Postman collections.

Install Required Plugins

Once Jenkins is installed, you need to install the necessary plugins. Install the "NodeJS" and "GitHub" plugins, which will be used to execute the Postman collections and fetch the code from your GitHub repository.

Configure Jenkins

Configure Jenkins by creating a new pipeline project. In the pipeline configuration, define the following stages:

- Checkout: This stage will fetch the code from your GitHub repository using the git command.
- Install: This stage will install Newman on the Jenkins machine using the npm command.
- Test: This stage will execute the Postman Collection using Newman, with the newman command.

The given below procedure is an example of a pipeline configuration:

```
pipeline {
  agent any

  stages {
   stage('Checkout') {
    steps {
     git 'https://github.com/username/repo.git'
     }
    }

   stage('Install') {
    steps {
     nodejs(nodeJSInstallationName: 'node') {
      sh 'npm install -g newman'
      }
     }
    }

   stage('Test') {
    steps {
     sh 'newman run /path/to/your/collection.json'
     }
```

```
      }
   }
}
```

Replace https://github.com/username/repo.git with the URL of your GitHub repository, and /path/to/your/collection.json with the actual path to your Postman Collection.

Schedule the Pipeline

Finally, schedule the pipeline to run on a regular basis, such as daily or weekly. This can be done using the Jenkins UI or the Jenkinsfile, which is the file that defines the pipeline.

The given below is an example of a Jenkinsfile that schedules the pipeline to run every day at 2am:

```
pipeline {
  agent any

  triggers {
    cron('0 2 * * *')
  }

  stages {
    // Define stages as before
  }
}
```

This will run the pipeline every day at 2am, without the need for manual intervention. Automating Postman collections involves running the collections on a scheduled basis, without the need for manual intervention. This can be accomplished using various tools and services, such as Jenkins, CircleCI, or Travis CI. By automating your Postman collections, you can ensure that your APIs are thoroughly tested and integrated on a regular basis, improving the quality, performance, and reliability of your APIs.

Chapter 7: API Documentation & Publishing

Importance of API Documentation

Postman is a popular and powerful API (Application Programming Interface) development tool used by developers and testers to design, develop, test, and debug APIs. Postman allows developers to create and maintain API documentation, making it easy for users to understand and work with APIs. In this section, we will discuss the features and benefits of Postman API documentation in detail.

Automatic Documentation Generation

Postman automatically generates API documentation based on your API collections. This live documentation updates as you make changes to your API, ensuring that your documentation remains accurate and up-to-date. You can also customize the generated documentation by adding descriptions, code snippets, and examples to provide comprehensive information about your API.

Markdown Support

Postman supports Markdown, a lightweight markup language for creating formatted text. This feature enables you to add rich text, images, and code snippets to your API documentation. You can format descriptions, provide examples, and enhance the readability of your API documentation using Markdown syntax.

Collaboration and Sharing

Postman's collaboration features allow you to share your API documentation with your team members and other stakeholders. You can publish the documentation to a custom URL or embed it in your website or application. Additionally, Postman allows you to share your API documentation through a public or private link, making it accessible to specific users or teams.

Versioning

Postman supports versioning, enabling you to maintain different versions of your API documentation. You can create new versions or update existing ones as your API evolves, ensuring that your documentation remains in sync with the changes. Versioning allows you to maintain historical records and provide access to previous versions of your API documentation if needed.

Code Snippets and SDK Generation

Postman can generate code snippets in multiple programming languages (such as Python,

JavaScript, and Ruby) based on your API requests. You can include these code snippets in your API documentation, making it easy for developers to understand and use your API in their applications. Additionally, Postman can generate SDKs (Software Development Kits) for your API, providing developers with pre-built libraries and tools for interacting with your API.

Customization and Theming

Postman allows you to customize the appearance of your API documentation to match your brand's visual identity. You can change the color scheme, fonts, and other elements of your documentation's layout to create a consistent look and feel. This customization enhances the user experience and helps promote brand recognition.

Interactive Documentation

Postman's API documentation is interactive, allowing users to send requests and view responses directly from the documentation. This feature makes it easy for users to test and explore your API without the need for additional tools or setup. Interactive documentation helps users understand your API's functionality and improves their overall experience.

Integration with CI/CD Pipelines

Postman API documentation can be integrated with your CI/CD (Continuous Integration/Continuous Deployment) pipelines to ensure that your documentation remains up-to-date as your API evolves. By automating the documentation update process, you can save time, reduce manual effort, and ensure that your documentation is always accurate.

Environments and Variables

Postman supports the use of environments and variables, allowing you to manage different configurations for your API documentation. You can define environment-specific variables (such as API keys, access tokens, and base URLs) and use them in your API requests and documentation. This feature simplifies configuration management and makes it easy to switch between different environments.

Access Control and Security

Postman offers access control and security features to protect your API documentation. You can restrict access to your documentation using role-based permissions, ensuring that only authorized users can view or edit the content. Additionally, Postman provides options to secure your API documentation using password protection or using API keys, ensuring that your sensitive information remains secure.

Monitoring and Analytics

Postman provides monitoring and analytics features to help you track the usage of your API documentation. You can monitor user engagement, view usage statistics, and gain insights into how your API is being used. This data can help you identify trends, improve your API's performance, and optimize your documentation for better user experience.

API Mock Servers

Postman allows you to create mock servers for your APIs, enabling you to simulate API responses and test your API documentation without the need for a live backend. This feature is particularly useful during the development phase when the backend is not yet ready or during maintenance periods. Mock servers help developers and testers to work concurrently and accelerate the development process.

Import and Export

Postman supports importing and exporting API documentation in various formats such as OpenAPI, RAML, and WSDL. This feature allows you to easily migrate your existing API documentation to Postman or integrate Postman with other tools and platforms. By supporting multiple formats, Postman ensures seamless compatibility and interoperability with different API documentation standards.

Multi-platform Support

Postman is available on multiple platforms, including Windows, macOS, and Linux, ensuring that your API documentation can be accessed and managed from any operating system. This cross-platform compatibility ensures that your team members can work with your API documentation, regardless of their preferred platform.

To summarize, Postman API documentation is a robust, feature-rich solution that simplifies the process of creating, managing, and sharing API documentation. Its automatic documentation generation, collaboration features, versioning, and customization options make it an essential tool for developers and testers. By using Postman API documentation, you can ensure that your APIs are well-documented, easy to understand, and accessible to your users, ultimately leading to better adoption and success of your APIs.

Automate Generating API Documentation

Generating and automating API documentation in Postman is a straightforward process. Follow the steps below to generate documentation for your collections and automate the process:

Create Collection

- Open Postman and click on the 'New' button in the top left corner.

- Choose 'Collection' from the dropdown menu.

- Enter a name and description for your collection, and click 'Create'.

Add Requests to the Collection

- Within the collection, click on the ellipsis (three dots) on the right side, and choose 'Add Request' from the dropdown menu.

- Enter a name for your request and click 'Save'.

- Choose the appropriate HTTP method (GET, POST, PUT, etc.) from the dropdown menu next to the request URL.

- Enter the request URL and any required parameters, headers, or body content.

- Click 'Send' to test your request.

- After receiving the expected response, click 'Save' to save the request to your collection.

Add Descriptions and Examples

- Click on the request in your collection.

- In the request pane, click on the 'Descriptions' tab.

- Use Markdown syntax to format your description, and click 'Save'.

- Click on the 'Examples' tab in the response pane.

- Click 'Save as example' and enter a name for the example. You can add multiple examples if needed.

Generate API Documentation

- Click on the ellipsis (three dots) next to your collection, and choose 'View documentation' from the dropdown menu.

- Postman will generate the API documentation based on your collection. You can customize the documentation by clicking on the 'Edit' button in the top right corner.

- To change the appearance, click on the 'Settings' tab and customize the color scheme, fonts, and other elements.

Publish and Share API Documentation

- Click on the 'Publish' button in the top right corner of the API documentation.

- Choose a version and environment for your API documentation.

- Click 'Publish Collection'.

- Share the generated URL with your team members or stakeholders, or embed the API documentation in your website or application.

Automate API Documentation Updates

To automate API documentation updates, you can integrate Postman with your CI/CD pipeline using the Postman API or the Newman CLI tool.

- Postman API: You can use the Postman API to programmatically update your collections and documentation. To obtain an API key, go to your Postman dashboard, click on your avatar in the top right corner, and choose 'Account Settings'. Then, navigate to the 'Postman API Keys' tab and generate a new API key.
- Newman CLI tool: Newman is a command-line tool that allows you to run Postman collections and update documentation. To install Newman, run npm install -g newman in your terminal or command prompt. Once installed, you can use Newman commands to run your collections and update your documentation.

With these steps, you can generate, customize, and automate your API documentation in

Postman, making it easy for your users to understand and work with your APIs.

Edit API Documentation

Editing an existing API documentation in Postman is simple. Following is a step-by-step walkthrough to help you edit your API documentation:

Access the API Documentation

- Open Postman and navigate to the 'Collections' tab on the left sidebar.

- Locate the collection containing the API documentation you want to edit.

- Click on the ellipsis (three dots) next to the collection name, and choose 'View documentation' from the dropdown menu.

Edit the API Documentation

- In the documentation view, click the 'Edit' button in the top right corner.

- You can now edit the following elements of your API documentation:
  - Collection Name and Description: Click on the collection name or description to edit them. Use Markdown syntax for formatting and styling your text.
  - Request Name and Description: Click on a request in the left sidebar to edit its name and description. Use Markdown syntax for formatting and styling your text.
  - Request Parameters, Headers, and Body: Click on the 'Params', 'Headers', or 'Body' tabs in the request pane to edit the corresponding details. Add or modify the parameters, headers, or body content as needed.
  - Response Examples: In the response pane, click on the 'Examples' tab. You can edit the existing examples or add new ones by clicking 'Save as example'. Provide a name for the example and edit the response content.

Save Your Changes

- After editing your API documentation, click the 'Save' button in the top right corner.

- If you've made changes to the collection name or description, click on the 'Update' button in the collection pane to save your changes.

<u>Update the Published Documentation (Optional)</u>

- If you've previously published your API documentation, you'll need to update the published version to reflect your recent changes.

- In the documentation view, click the 'Publish' button in the top right corner.

- Review the changes you've made and click the 'Update' button to update the published documentation.

By following the practical steps outlined for managing API policies and standards in Postman, you can easily edit and update your existing API documentation. It is important to save your changes and update the published documentation regularly to ensure that your users have access to the most recent version of your API documentation. This ensures that your users have access to accurate and up-to-date information about your APIs.

Publish, Unpublish and Modify Documentation

Assuming you have already created a collection with API documentation in Postman, you can easily publish it to make it available to your API consumers. You can then modify the documentation as needed, and unpublish it when it is no longer relevant or accurate. This process ensures that your API documentation is up-to-date and accessible to your API consumers.

The given below procedure is a step-by-step walkthrough for each action:

<u>Publish the API Documentation</u>

Access the API Documentation
- Open Postman and navigate to the 'Collections' tab on the left sidebar.

- Locate the collection containing the API documentation you want to publish.

- Click on the ellipsis (three dots) next to the collection name, and choose 'View documentation' from the dropdown menu.

Publish the API Documentation
- In the documentation view, click the 'Publish' button in the top right corner.

- Select a version and environment for your API documentation. You can also customize the appearance of your documentation under the 'Settings' tab.

Click 'Publish Collection'.

After publishing, you'll be provided with a URL for your API documentation. Share this URL with your team members, stakeholders, or embed it in your website or application.

Modify the Published API Documentation

Edit the API Documentation (as described in the previous section)
- In the documentation view, click the 'Edit' button in the top right corner.

- Edit the desired elements of your API documentation (e.g., collection name, request description, response examples, etc.).

- Click the 'Save' button in the top right corner to save your changes.

Update the Published API Documentation
- In the documentation view, click the 'Publish' button in the top right corner.

- Review the changes you've made and click the 'Update' button to update the published documentation. This will ensure that the published version reflects your recent changes.

Unpublish API Documentation

Access the Published API Documentation
- In the documentation view, click the 'Publish' button in the top right corner.

Unpublish the API Documentation
- In the 'Publish Collection' window, scroll down to the 'Unpublish' section.

- Click the 'Unpublish' button. A confirmation dialog will appear.

- Click 'Unpublish' again in the confirmation dialog to remove the published documentation. The API documentation will no longer be accessible via the previously generated URL.

By publishing your API documentation in Postman, you make it easily accessible to your API consumers, improving their ability to consume your APIs. With Postman, you can modify your API documentation as needed, and unpublish it when necessary. It's important to keep your API documentation up-to-date and accurate, and to publish it only when it meets your organization's quality, security, and performance standards. By updating your published documentation regularly, you ensure that your users have access to the most recent version of your API documentation, helping to improve their experience and satisfaction with your API program.

Publishing APIs on GitHub

Postman offers integrations with popular documentation platforms such as Swagger and API Blueprint, allowing you to export your API documentation directly from Postman and publish it on various platforms. This automation saves you time and effort and ensures that your API documentation remains up-to-date and consistent across all platforms. With just a few clicks, you can share your API documentation with your team members, API consumers, and other stakeholders, making it easily accessible and understandable.

The given below procedure is a step-by-step walkthrough on how to publish your API documentation on GitHub Pages, a popular platform for hosting static websites:

Export the API Documentation

- In Postman, navigate to the 'Collections' tab on the left sidebar.

- Click on the ellipsis (three dots) next to the collection containing the API documentation you want to publish.

- Choose 'Export' from the dropdown menu.

- Select the desired format for your documentation (e.g., HTML, Markdown, JSON), and choose a location to save the exported file.

Create GitHub Pages Repository

- Go to GitHub.com and sign in to your account.

- Create a new repository by clicking on the 'New' button in the top left corner of the dashboard.

- Choose a name for your repository, and ensure that it is set to public.

- Check the 'Initialize this repository with a README' box, and click 'Create Repository'.

Clone Repository to Local Machine

- On the repository page, click on the 'Code' button, and copy the HTTPS URL provided.

- Open a terminal or command prompt on your local machine, and navigate to the desired directory where you want to clone the repository.

- Run the command git clone <HTTPS URL> and replace <HTTPS URL> with the URL you copied earlier.

Add API Documentation to Repository

- Move the exported API documentation file to the cloned repository directory on your local machine.

- In the terminal or command prompt, navigate to the repository directory.

- Run the command git add . to stage all changes in the repository.

- Run the command git commit -m "Added API documentation" to commit the changes to the repository.

Push Changes to GitHub

- Run the command git push to upload the changes to GitHub.

- Enter your GitHub credentials if prompted.

Configure GitHub Pages

- On the repository page, click on the 'Settings' tab.

- Scroll down to the 'GitHub Pages' section and select the branch that contains your API documentation file. For example, if your file is named index.html and is located in the master branch, select master from the dropdown menu.

- Click 'Save'.

Access the Published API Documentation

- On the repository page, click on the link provided under the 'GitHub Pages' section to access your published API documentation.

By following these steps, you can publish your API documentation on GitHub Pages. You can also use similar integration features to publish your documentation on other platforms, such as AWS S3, Azure Blob Storage, or your own web server. By automating the process of exporting and publishing your API documentation, you can save time and ensure that your users have easy access to your documentation, regardless of the platform they use.

Publishing APIs on GitLab

If you want to share your API documentation on GitLab, you can easily do so by utilizing GitLab Pages. This convenient built-in feature enables you to host static websites straight from your GitLab repository. By publishing your API documentation on GitLab Pages, you can make it accessible to your team members, clients, and other stakeholders. Plus, since it's hosted on GitLab, you can easily manage and update the documentation as needed.

The given below procedure is a step-by-step walkthrough on how to publish your API documentation on GitLab Pages:

Export the API Documentation

- In Postman, navigate to the 'Collections' tab on the left sidebar.

- Click on the ellipsis (three dots) next to the collection containing the API documentation you want to publish.

- Choose 'Export' from the dropdown menu.

- Select the desired format for your documentation (e.g., HTML, Markdown, JSON), and choose a location to save the exported file.

Create GitLab Repository

- Go to GitLab.com and sign in to your account.

- Create a new project by clicking on the '+' button in the top right corner of the dashboard.

- Choose a name for your project, and ensure that it is set to public.

- Check the 'Initialize repository with a README' box, and click 'Create Project'.

Clone Repository to Local Machine

- On the repository page, copy the HTTPS URL provided.

- Open a terminal or command prompt on your local machine, and navigate to the desired directory where you want to clone the repository.

- Run the command git clone <HTTPS URL> and replace <HTTPS URL> with the URL you copied earlier.

Add API Documentation to Repository

- Move the exported API documentation file to the cloned repository directory on your local machine.

- In the terminal or command prompt, navigate to the repository directory.

- Run the command git add . to stage all changes in the repository.

- Run the command git commit -m "Added API documentation" to commit the changes to the repository.

Push Changes to GitLab

- Run the command git push to upload the changes to GitLab.

- Enter your GitLab credentials if prompted.

Configure GitLab Pages

- On the repository page, click on the 'Settings' tab.

- Scroll down to the 'Pages' section and select the branch that contains your API documentation file. For example, if your file is named index.html and is located in the master branch, select master from the dropdown menu.

- In the 'Domain' field, enter a subdomain for your API documentation. For example, if you enter myapi, your documentation will be accessible at https://myusername.gitlab.io/myapi/.

- Click 'Save Changes'.

Access the Published API Documentation

- On the repository page, click on the 'Pages' tab.

- Click on the link provided to access your published API documentation.

By following these steps, you can publish your API documentation on GitLab Pages. You can also use similar integration features to publish your documentation on other platforms, such as GitHub Pages, AWS S3, Azure Blob Storage, or your own web server. By automating the process of exporting and publishing your API documentation, you can save time and ensure that your users have easy access to your documentation, regardless of the platform they use.

Publishing APIs on Bitbucket

The given below procedure is a step-by-step walkthrough on how to publish your API documentation on Bitbucket Pages:

Export the API Documentation

- In Postman, navigate to the 'Collections' tab on the left sidebar.

- Click on the ellipsis (three dots) next to the collection containing the API documentation you want to publish.

- Choose 'Export' from the dropdown menu.

- Select the desired format for your documentation (e.g., HTML, Markdown, JSON), and choose a location to save the exported file.

Create Bitbucket Repository

- Go to Bitbucket.org and sign in to your account.

- Create a new repository by clicking on the '+' button in the top right corner of the dashboard.

- Choose a name for your repository, and ensure that it is set to public.

- Check the 'Initialize repository' box, and click 'Create Repository'.

Clone Repository to Local Machine

- On the repository page, copy the HTTPS URL provided.

- Open a terminal or command prompt on your local machine, and navigate to the desired directory where you want to clone the repository.

- Run the command git clone <HTTPS URL> and replace <HTTPS URL> with the URL you copied earlier.

Add API Documentation to Repository

- Move the exported API documentation file to the cloned repository directory on your local machine.

- In the terminal or command prompt, navigate to the repository directory.

- Run the command git add . to stage all changes in the repository.

- Run the command git commit -m "Added API documentation" to commit the changes to the repository.

Push Changes to Bitbucket

- Run the command git push to upload the changes to Bitbucket.

- Enter your Bitbucket credentials if prompted.

Configure Bitbucket Pages

- On the repository page, click on the 'Settings' tab.

- Scroll down to the 'Bitbucket Pages' section and select the branch that contains your API documentation file. For example, if your file is named index.html and is located in the master branch, select master from the dropdown menu.

- In the 'Path' field, enter a subdirectory for your API documentation. For example, if you enter myapi, your documentation will be accessible at https://myusername.bitbucket.io/myapi/.

- Click 'Save'.

Access the Published API Documentation

- On the repository page, click on the 'Bitbucket Pages' tab.

- Click on the link provided to access your published API documentation.

By following these steps, you can publish your API documentation on Bitbucket Pages. You can also use similar integration features to publish your documentation on other platforms, such as GitHub Pages, GitLab Pages, AWS S3, Azure Blob Storage, or your own web server. By automating the process of exporting and publishing your API documentation, you can save time and ensure that your users have easy access to your documentation, regardless of the platform they use.

Managing API Versions and Changes

In Postman, managing documentation for different API versions requires a systematic approach. You need to create collections for each version of your API and organize them in a structured way. Once the collections are set up, you should update the documentation to reflect the changes made to each API version. This helps to ensure that your documentation is accurate and up-to-date, making it easier for users to understand the different API versions and how they can interact with them. Overall, proper documentation management in Postman can help you streamline your API development process and improve communication with your users.

The given below procedure is a step-by-step walkthrough on how to manage API documentation for multiple versions:

Create Collections for Each API Version

- In Postman, navigate to the 'Collections' tab on the left sidebar.

- Click the 'New' button in the top left corner, and choose 'Collection' from the dropdown menu.

- Enter a name for your collection (e.g., "My API v1") and a description, then click 'Create'.

- Repeat this process for each API version you want to manage (e.g., "My API v2", "My API v3", etc.).

Add Requests and Documentation for Each Version

- For each collection, add requests and document them as described in previous responses.

- Ensure that you accurately document the unique features, parameters, and responses of each API version.

Publish API Documentation for Each Version

- For each collection, follow the steps outlined in the previous response to publish the API documentation.

- Make sure to select the appropriate version and environment for each collection.

- Keep track of the generated URLs for each published API documentation version.

Update API Documentation for Each Version

- If you need to make changes to the API documentation for a specific version, edit the corresponding collection and update the published documentation as described in previous responses.

- Remember to republish the documentation to reflect the changes made.

Organize and Share Versioned API Documentation

To make it easier for users to find and navigate between different versions of your API documentation, you can create a central index or landing page that lists all available versions.

- Create a separate web page or a Markdown file to serve as an index or landing page for your API documentation.

- Add a brief introduction to your API and list all available API versions with links to their corresponding published API documentation URLs.

- Optionally, include a section on your index or landing page to provide information on the differences between the versions, migration guides, or any other relevant details.

- Share the index or landing page URL with your users to help them find and navigate between the different versions of your API documentation.

Managing and organizing API documentation for multiple versions can be a challenging task, especially when dealing with complex APIs. However, by following the above couple of simple steps, you can efficiently manage your API documentation. This approach involves creating separate collections for each API version, using descriptive names and labels, and adding relevant information and documentation to each version. By doing so, you can ensure that users have access to accurate and up-to-date information for the version of the API they are working with, which can help improve their experience and save time. Overall, effective API documentation management is essential for ensuring the success of your API and the satisfaction of your users.

API Publishing Best Practices

To ensure successful API publishing, follow best practices such as thoroughly documenting APIs, providing developer support, and ensuring API security and scalability for efficient performance. Below are:

Document Your API

Good documentation is critical to the success of your API. Developers rely on documentation to understand how to use an API and integrate it into their applications. Your API documentation should include all the necessary information, such as the endpoints, parameters, responses, and error codes. Use clear and concise language, and provide examples and code snippets to help developers understand how to use your API. Ensure that your documentation is up-to-date and reflects any changes made to your API.

Use Versioning

As your API evolves, you may need to make changes that are not backwards-compatible. To avoid breaking existing integrations, use versioning to manage changes and allow developers to choose the version of the API they want to use. By versioning your API, you can ensure that developers who rely on your API can continue to use it without interruption, even as you make changes and improvements.

Secure Your API

APIs are often targeted by attackers, so it's important to implement proper security measures. Use authentication and authorization to restrict access to your API, and use encryption to protect data in transit. Implementing security measures is crucial to protect user data and prevent unauthorized access or misuse of your API. As the owner of the API, it's your responsibility to ensure that your users' data is protected.

Test Your API

Before publishing your API, make sure to thoroughly test it to ensure that it works as expected. Use automated testing tools to catch issues early on and reduce the risk of introducing bugs in production. By testing your API, you can ensure that it functions correctly and meets the needs of your users. Thorough testing can prevent costly errors and downtime, which can negatively impact the user experience.

Monitor Your API

After publishing your API, monitor it regularly to ensure that it is performing well and meeting the needs of your users. Use analytics tools to track usage patterns and identify areas for improvement. By monitoring your API, you can identify any performance issues and make necessary changes to improve its functionality. You can also use the data collected to identify trends and patterns in user behavior, which can help you improve the API's functionality and meet users' needs more effectively.

Provide Support

When developers encounter issues with your API, they will need support to resolve them. Provide clear and responsive support channels, such as a forum, email, or chat, and respond to queries promptly. By providing support, you can help developers integrate your API into their applications more effectively, reducing the likelihood of issues and improving the user experience.

Follow Industry Standards

To ensure interoperability and ease of integration, follow industry standards and conventions when designing and publishing your API. Use common data formats, such as JSON or XML, and follow RESTful design principles. By following these standards, you can ensure that your API is easy to use and integrates seamlessly with other applications.

Overall, creating a successful API requires careful planning, design, and execution. By following the above enlisted best practices for API development, including documentation, versioning, security, testing, monitoring, support, and adherence to industry standards, you can create a reliable and effective API that meets the needs of your users. A well-designed and maintained API can help you attract and retain users, improve the user experience, and promote the success of your application or business.

CHAPTER 8: API INTEGRATION

Understand API Integration

API integration refers to the process of connecting different software applications or systems via APIs (Application Programming Interfaces) in order to exchange data or functionality. APIs are interfaces that allow different software programs to communicate with each other, and API integration involves using these interfaces to connect systems and enable them to share data and functionality seamlessly.

Integration to Different Systems

When it comes to integrating your APIs with other systems, there are a variety of options available to you.

The given below are some of the most common systems that you can integrate your APIs with:

- Mobile Applications: One of the most popular use cases for APIs is integrating them into mobile applications. APIs can enable your mobile app to retrieve data from your backend systems and present it to users in real-time.
- Web Applications: APIs can also be integrated into web applications, allowing you to retrieve data and functionality from other systems and present it to users within your web application.
- Cloud Services: APIs can be integrated with various cloud services like AWS, Google Cloud, Azure, etc. to enable you to utilize their services and functionalities in your own application or system.
- IoT Devices: APIs can be integrated with IoT (Internet of Things) devices, allowing you to retrieve and analyze data from sensors or control and monitor devices remotely.
- Enterprise Applications: APIs can be integrated with other enterprise applications like CRM, ERP, and SCM systems to streamline business processes and improve operational efficiency.

Process of API Integration

The process of integrating APIs involves several steps, including:

- Identifying the systems you want to integrate: The first step is to identify the systems you want to integrate with your APIs. This involves understanding the business requirements and objectives of the integration.
- Choosing the integration method: Once you've identified the systems you want to integrate, you need to choose the integration method that best suits your needs. This could involve using middleware, webhooks, or custom integration solutions.
- Mapping data and functionality: The next step is to map the data and functionality

you want to share between the systems. This involves defining the data elements and functionality that need to be shared, and creating the necessary mappings and transformations.

- Implementing the integration: Once you've mapped the data and functionality, you need to implement the integration by creating the necessary APIs, middleware, and other integration components.
- Testing and validation: Finally, you need to test and validate the integration to ensure that it's working as expected and meeting your business requirements.

Overall, API integration is a critical process for modern software development, as it enables you to connect different systems and streamline business processes. By understanding the different systems you can integrate with and following best practices for integration, you can ensure that your APIs are integrated effectively and efficiently.

Sample Program to Integrate OpenWeatherMap API

Let's say we want to integrate with the OpenWeatherMap API to retrieve the current weather data for a specific city. The given below are the steps we can follow:

Identify the API endpoint: The OpenWeatherMap API has a REST endpoint for retrieving weather data, which we can use for our integration. The endpoint URL is https://api.openweathermap.org/data/2.5/weather.

Create a new request: In Postman, we can create a new request by clicking on the "New" button on the top left corner of the application and selecting the "GET" request type from the dropdown menu.

Enter the API endpoint: In the request editor, we can enter the API endpoint URL https://api.openweathermap.org/data/2.5/weather in the "Enter request URL" field.

Add headers and authorization: The OpenWeatherMap API requires an API key to access the data. We can add this key to our request by clicking on the "Headers" tab in the request editor and adding a new header with the key appid and the value of our API key. For example, appid: YOUR_API_KEY.

Enter request parameters: The OpenWeatherMap API allows us to retrieve weather data for a specific city by passing a q parameter with the name of the city in the request URL. We can enter this parameter in the "Params" tab by adding a new key-value pair with the key q and the value of the city name. For example, q: London.

Send the request: Once we've set up our request, we can send it by clicking on the "Send" button in the request editor. Postman will send the request to the OpenWeatherMap API and display the response in the "Response" pane.

Validate the response: In the response pane, we can see the weather data for the city of London in JSON format. We can use Postman's built-in tools to validate the data, such as checking the status code, response time, and response body.

The given below is an example of the code you can use in Postman to retrieve weather data for a specific city using the OpenWeatherMap API:

```
// Set the API endpoint URL
const apiUrl = "https://api.openweathermap.org/data/2.5/weather";

// Set the API key
const apiKey = "YOUR_API_KEY";

// Set the city name
const cityName = "London";

// Set up the request
pm.sendRequest({
  url: apiUrl,
  method: 'GET',
  header: {
    'Content-Type': 'application/json',
    'appid': apiKey
  },
  params: {
    'q': cityName
  }
}, function (err, response) {
  // Handle any errors
  if (err) {
```

```
        console.log(err);
        return;
    }

    // Retrieve the response data
    const responseData = response.json();

    // Validate the response data
    console.log("Response status code: " + response.code);
    console.log("Response time: " + response.responseTime + "ms");
    console.log("Temperature: " + responseData.main.temp);
    console.log("Humidity: " + responseData.main.humidity);
    console.log("Weather description: " + responseData.weather[0].description);
});
```

In the above demonstrated program, we're setting the API endpoint URL, API key, and city name as variables. We're then using the pm.sendRequest() function to send a GET request to the OpenWeatherMap API with the appropriate headers and parameters. Finally, we're validating the response data by logging the status code, response time, temperature, humidity, and weather description to the console. By using this code in Postman, you can easily retrieve weather data for any city using the OpenWeatherMap API and validate the response data to ensure that it's accurate.

Data and Functionality Mapping

Overview

Mapping data and functionality is an important step in API integration, as it involves defining the data elements and functionality that need to be shared between systems. In the case of the OpenWeatherMap API, we can map the data and functionality as follows:

Data Elements

The OpenWeatherMap API returns weather data for a specific city in JSON format. We can map the data elements we want to retrieve from the API, such as the current temperature, humidity, wind speed, and weather description. For example, we can access the temperature data using the main.temp property in the JSON response.

Functionality

The OpenWeatherMap API allows us to retrieve weather data for a specific city by passing a q parameter with the name of the city in the request URL. We can map this functionality to our own application or system by providing a user interface where users can enter the name of a city and retrieve the current weather data.

Steps to Map Data and Functionality

To integrate the OpenWeatherMap API using Postman and map the data and functionality, we can follow these steps:

- Create a new request in Postman and enter the API endpoint URL: https://api.openweathermap.org/data/2.5/weather
  - Add an appid header with your API key to authenticate the request. You can do this by clicking on the "Headers" tab and adding a new header with the key appid and the value of your API key.
  - Enter the q parameter with the name of the city you want to retrieve weather data for. You can do this by clicking on the "Params" tab and adding a new key-value pair with the key q and the value of the city name.
  - Send the request and retrieve the JSON response. You can do this by clicking on the "Send" button in the request editor and reviewing the response in the "Response" pane.
  - Map the data elements you want to retrieve from the JSON response. For example, if you want to retrieve the current temperature data, you can access the main.temp property in the JSON response.
  - Map the functionality you want to provide to your users. For example, you can provide a user interface where users can enter the name of a city and retrieve the current weather data using the OpenWeatherMap API.

By mapping the data elements and functionality of the OpenWeatherMap API in this way, we can integrate the API into our own application or system and provide real-time weather data to our users.

Test and Validate API Integration

testing and validating your API integration is a critical step in ensuring that your application or system is working as expected. There are several techniques you can use to test and validate your API integration using Postman. The given below are some examples:

Manual Testing

Manual testing involves manually sending requests to the API endpoint using Postman and reviewing the response data. This can be done by creating a new request in Postman and entering the API endpoint URL, headers, and parameters. Once you've sent the request, you can review the response in the "Response" pane and validate that the data is correct.

Following are the steps to perform manual testing:
- Create a new request in Postman and enter the API endpoint URL https://api.openweathermap.org/data/2.5/weather.
- Add an appid header with your API key to authenticate the request. You can do this by clicking on the "Headers" tab and adding a new header with the key appid and the value of your API key.
- Enter the q parameter with the name of the city you want to retrieve weather data for. You can do this by clicking on the "Params" tab and adding a new key-value pair with the key q and the value of the city name.
- Send the request and retrieve the JSON response. You can do this by clicking on the "Send" button in the request editor and reviewing the response in the "Response" pane.
- Validate the response data manually. For example, you can check that the response status code is 200 OK, the response time is within an acceptable range, and the response data contains the expected data elements (e.g. temperature, humidity, wind speed, etc.).

<u>Sample Program of Manual Testing</u>

The given below is an example of how you can validate the response data manually:

```
// Send the request
pm.sendRequest({
    url: "https://api.openweathermap.org/data/2.5/weather",
    method: 'GET',
    header: {
        'Content-Type': 'application/json',
        'appid': 'YOUR_API_KEY'
    },
    params: {
        'q': 'London'
    }
}, function (err, response) {
```

```
// Handle any errors
if (err) {
  console.log(err);
  return;
}


// Retrieve the response data
const responseData = response.json();


// Validate the response data manually
console.log("Response status code: " + response.code);
console.log("Response time: " + response.responseTime + "ms");
console.log("Temperature: " + responseData.main.temp);
console.log("Humidity: " + responseData.main.humidity);
console.log("Weather description: " + responseData.weather[0].description);
});
```

In the above demonstrated program, we're using the pm.sendRequest() function to send a GET request to the OpenWeatherMap API with the appropriate headers and parameters. We're then retrieving the response data and manually validating it by logging the status code, response time, temperature, humidity, and weather description to the console. By using this code in Postman, you can easily manually test your API integration and ensure that it's working as expected.

Automated Testing

Automated testing involves creating automated test scripts in Postman that can be run automatically to validate your API integration. This can be done using Postman's built-in testing framework, which allows you to write JavaScript code to perform tests and assertions on the response data.

Following are the steps to perform automated testing:
- Create a new request in Postman and enter the API endpoint URL https://api.openweathermap.org/data/2.5/weather.
- Add an appid header with your API key to authenticate the request. You can do this by clicking on the "Headers" tab and adding a new header with the key appid

and the value of your API key.

- Enter the q parameter with the name of the city you want to retrieve weather data for. You can do this by clicking on the "Params" tab and adding a new key-value pair with the key q and the value of the city name.
- Send the request and retrieve the JSON response. You can do this by clicking on the "Send" button in the request editor and reviewing the response in the "Response" pane.
- Validate the response data manually. For example, you can check that the response status code is 200 OK, the response time is within an acceptable range, and the response data contains the expected data elements (e.g. temperature, humidity, wind speed, etc.).

Sample Program of Automated Testing

The given below is an example of an automated test script for the OpenWeatherMap API integration:

```
pm.test("Status code is 200", function () {
    pm.response.to.have.status(200);
});


pm.test("Response time is less than 200ms", function () {
    pm.expect(pm.response.responseTime).to.be.below(200);
});

pm.test("Temperature is a number", function () {
    pm.expect(typeof pm.response.json().main.temp).to.eql("number");
});

pm.test("City name is London", function () {
    pm.expect(pm.response.json().name).to.eql("London");
});

pm.test("Humidity is between 0 and 100", function () {
    pm.expect(pm.response.json().main.humidity).to.be.within(0, 100);
```

```javascript
});
```

In the above demonstrated program, we're testing several aspects of the response data, including the status code, response time, temperature, city name, and humidity.

CHAPTER 9: API PERFORMANCE

Explore API Performance

API performance refers to the speed, reliability, and efficiency of how an application program interface (API) works. It plays a crucial role in the overall success of any software development project. An API that delivers high performance can improve user experience, enhance productivity, and increase customer satisfaction.

Why Measuring API Performance?

The importance of API performance can be understood by the fact that it directly impacts the end-users of the application. A slow, unreliable, or inefficient API can cause delays in executing user requests, leading to frustration and dissatisfaction. Moreover, in today's fast-paced digital world, users have a low tolerance for slow and unreliable systems, and they are likely to abandon an application that doesn't perform well.

The importance of API performance can be further elaborated as follows:

User Experience:

The API is the backbone of any software application. The speed and responsiveness of an API directly impact the user experience. If the API is slow or unresponsive, users will have a negative experience, leading to a loss of customers.

Business Performance:

The success of any software project is measured by its business performance. APIs play a critical role in the performance of the application. A high-performance API can result in improved productivity, faster processing times, and increased revenue.

Scalability:

APIs should be designed to handle increasing loads as the application grows. If the API is not scalable, it will lead to a bottleneck, resulting in performance degradation.

Reliability:

APIs should be designed to handle errors gracefully. A reliable API will return appropriate error messages that help developers quickly identify and fix issues.

Postman Performance Capabilities

Postman is an API testing and development tool that provides several features that help to ensure high API performance. Some of these features include:

Automated Testing:

Postman provides a powerful framework for automated API testing. With this feature, developers can create and run automated tests to validate API functionality and performance. Automated testing helps to identify performance issues before they impact users, allowing developers to fix issues proactively. By automating the testing process, developers can quickly and easily identify bugs and performance issues and address them before they become bigger problems.

Load Testing:

Postman provides load testing features that help to simulate high user loads on APIs. Load testing helps to identify performance bottlenecks and ensure that APIs can handle high user loads. With this feature, developers can test the performance of their APIs under a variety of scenarios and identify areas that need optimization. Load testing helps to ensure that APIs can handle high traffic volumes and that the response time remains acceptable for users.

Real-Time Monitoring:

Postman provides real-time monitoring of APIs. This feature allows developers to track API performance metrics such as response time, error rate, and throughput in real-time. Real-time monitoring enables developers to identify and fix issues quickly. By monitoring the performance of their APIs in real-time, developers can identify and address performance issues proactively, before they become bigger problems.

Collaboration:

Postman provides collaboration features that allow multiple developers to work on the same API. Collaboration ensures that APIs are developed efficiently and that performance issues are addressed proactively. By collaborating on API development, developers can identify potential performance issues early on and address them before they become bigger problems. Collaboration also helps to ensure that APIs are well-documented and that developers have the resources they need to optimize performance.

Documentation:

Postman provides a comprehensive documentation feature that helps to ensure that APIs are well-documented. Good documentation helps to ensure that APIs are easy to use, and developers can quickly understand how to use them. By providing detailed documentation, developers can ensure that their APIs are used correctly, which can help to prevent performance issues. Documentation also helps to ensure that developers have the resources they need to optimize performance.

To summarize, Postman provides a suite of features that can help to identify and address performance issues in APIs. By using Postman's automated testing, load testing, real-time monitoring, collaboration, and documentation features, developers can proactively identify and address performance issues before they impact users. These features help to ensure that APIs perform optimally and provide a good user experience.

Measure API Performance

Measuring the performance of APIs is critical to ensure that they are providing a fast, reliable, and efficient service to the end-users. To monitor API performance, developers rely on a set of performance indicators or metrics that help them identify bottlenecks, track trends, and optimize the system's overall performance. In this section, We will enlist and explain some of the most important performance indicators to measure the performance of APIs.

Response Time

Response time is the amount of time it takes for an API to respond to a request from the client. This metric measures the end-to-end time it takes to complete a request and includes network latency, server processing time, and other overheads. Response time is one of the most critical performance indicators as it directly impacts user experience.

Measuring API Response Time

To measure the response time of your API, you can use the following code snippet in Python using the requests library:

```python
import requests
import time

start_time = time.time()
response = requests.get('https://your-api-endpoint.com')
end_time = time.time()

response_time = end_time - start_time
print("API Response Time: ", response_time)
```

This code sends a GET request to your API endpoint and measures the time it takes for the API to respond. The time module is used to calculate the difference between the start and end times, giving you the response time in seconds.

Error Rate

The error rate is the percentage of requests that result in an error. This metric measures the reliability of the API and its ability to handle errors gracefully. A high error rate indicates that there are issues with the API's functionality or configuration that need to be addressed.

Calculating API Error Rate

To measure the error rate of your API, you can use a tool like Postman to send multiple requests and track the error responses. Following is an example of how to measure the error rate using Postman:

- Create a collection of requests to your API endpoint in Postman.
- Run a load test on the collection, sending a high number of requests simultaneously.
- In the Postman console, you can view the error responses and calculate the error rate as a percentage of the total requests sent.

Alternatively, you can use Python to measure the error rate using the requests library:

```
import requests


response = requests.get('https://your-api-endpoint.com')
if response.status_code != 200:
    print("Error: ", response.status_code)
```

This code sends a GET request to your API endpoint and checks if the response code is not 200 (which indicates an error). You can then count the number of error responses and calculate the error rate as a percentage of the total requests sent.

Throughput

Throughput measures the number of requests that an API can handle per unit time. It is an essential metric for assessing the capacity of an API to handle high loads. High throughput is critical for applications with high traffic volumes.

Measuring API Throughput

To measure the throughput of your API, you can use a load testing tool like Apache JMeter.

Following is an example of how to measure throughput using JMeter:

- Create a test plan in JMeter with a Thread Group that simulates the number of concurrent users you expect to have.
- Add a HTTP Request sampler to the Thread Group with the API endpoint URL.
- Set the Ramp-Up Period to gradually increase the number of threads over time.
- Run the test and monitor the throughput in the Summary Report.

Alternatively, you can use Python to measure the throughput using the requests library:

```python
import requests
import time


start_time = time.time()
for i in range(100):
    response = requests.get('https://your-api-endpoint.com')
end_time = time.time()


total_time = end_time - start_time
throughput = 100 / total_time
print("API Throughput: ", throughput)
```

This code sends 100 GET requests to your API endpoint and calculates the time it took to complete all requests. The throughput is then calculated as the number of requests divided by the total time.

CPU/Memory Utilization

CPU Utilization measures the percentage of the CPU that is used by an API. High CPU utilization can lead to performance degradation and decreased response time. It is essential to monitor CPU utilization and ensure that it is optimized for efficient performance. Memory Utilization measures the amount of memory that an API is using. High memory utilization can lead to performance issues and system crashes. It is essential to monitor memory utilization and ensure that it is optimized for efficient performance.

Monitoring CPU and Memory Utilization

To measure CPU and memory utilization of your API, you can use monitoring tools like Prometheus and Grafana. Following is an example of how to set up Prometheus and

Grafana to monitor CPU and memory utilization:
- Install Prometheus and Grafana on your server.
- Configure Prometheus to collect CPU and memory usage data from your server.
- Create a Grafana dashboard with CPU and memory utilization metrics.
- Monitor the dashboard to track CPU and memory utilization.

Network Latency

Network Latency measures the amount of time it takes for a request to travel from the client to the server and back. High network latency can result in slower response times and a poor user experience. It is important to monitor network latency and optimize it for efficient performance.

Monitoring Network Latency

To measure network latency of your API, you can use the following code snippet in Python using the ping command:

```python
import os

hostname = 'your-api-endpoint.com'
response = os.system("ping -c 1 " + hostname)
if response == 0:
    print(hostname, 'is up!')
```

This code sends a ping request to your API endpoint and measures the round-trip time. The output will show the hostname and whether it's up or not. You can use this code to monitor the network latency of your API over time.

Error Response Time

Error Response Time measures the amount of time it takes for an API to respond to an error. This metric is critical for assessing the API's ability to handle errors gracefully and respond quickly to issues.

Calculating Error Response Time

To measure the error response time of your API, you can modify the code snippet in Step 2 above to measure the time it takes for an error response to be returned. Following is an example of how to do this in Python:

```python
import requests
import time

start_time = time.time()
response = requests.get('https://your-api-endpoint.com')
end_time = time.time()

if response.status_code != 200:
    error_response_time = end_time - start_time
    print("Error Response Time: ", error_response_time)
```

This code sends a GET request to your API endpoint and measures the time it takes for an error response to be returned (if the response code is not 200). You can use this code to monitor the error response time of your API over time.

Time to First Byte (TTFB)

TTFB measures the amount of time it takes for an API to start sending data after receiving a request. A slow TTFB can indicate issues with server processing time, network latency, or other performance bottlenecks.

Measuring TTFB

To measure the TTFB of your API, you can use a tool like Pingdom. Following is an example of how to measure TTFB using Pingdom:

- Create a Pingdom account and add your API endpoint to the list of monitored websites.
- Run a test on your API endpoint and view the results in the Performance tab.
- Look for the "Time to First Byte" metric, which measures the time it takes for the server to respond to the first byte of the request.

Alternatively, you can use Python to measure the TTFB using the requests library:

```python
import requests
```

```python
response = requests.get('https://your-api-endpoint.com')
ttfb = response.elapsed.total_seconds() -
response.elapsed.content.total_seconds()
print("Time to First Byte: ", ttfb)
```

This code sends a GET request to your API endpoint and measures the time it takes for the server to respond to the first byte of the request. The total_seconds() method is used to calculate the time in seconds.

To summarize, these are some practical ways to measure the key performance indicators of your APIs. By monitoring these KPIs, you can identify bottlenecks, track trends, and optimize the overall performance of your API.

Identify and Fix Performance Issues

Performance issues in APIs can cause slow response times, high error rates, and poor user experience. These issues can occur due to various factors, such as inefficient code, poor API architecture, and high user loads. Slow response times can be caused by network latency, database queries, or inefficient code. High error rates can be caused by bugs in the code or incorrect handling of user inputs. Poor user experience can result from slow response times, frequent errors, or poor documentation. To address performance issues, developers can optimize their API code, improve the API architecture, use caching and asynchronous processing, and monitor and optimize the API performance.

Response Time Issues

To identify performance issues related to response time in Postman, you can use the Collection Runner to run multiple requests simultaneously and measure the response time for each request.

The given below step-by-step procedure is how you can do this:
- Open your collection in Postman and click on the "Runner" button in the top-right corner.
- Select the environment and the collection that you want to run, and click on the "Run" button.
- Once the collection has finished running, you can view the response time for each request in the "Run Summary" tab.
- To set a threshold for response time, you can use industry-standard values as benchmarks. For example, Google recommends that web pages should load in

under 2 seconds. However, the response time for APIs can vary based on the complexity of the request and the server load. Therefore, you should establish an internal benchmark that reflects the expectations of your users and the nature of your API.

Sample Program to Detect Response Time Exceeding 2s

The given below is a sample program to check if the response time is higher than the threshold and print an error message if it is:

```python
import requests
import time

start_time = time.time()
response = requests.get('https://your-api-endpoint.com')
end_time = time.time()

response_time = end_time - start_time
threshold = 2  # set the threshold in seconds
if response_time > threshold:
    print("Error: Response Time exceeded threshold")
```

In the above sample program, if the response time exceeds the threshold of 2 seconds, an error message is printed.

Detect Higher Error Rate

To identify performance issues related to error rate in Postman, you can use the Collection Runner to run multiple requests and track the error rate for each request.

The given below step-by-step procedure is how you can do this:
- Open your collection in Postman and click on the "Runner" button in the top-right corner.
- Select the environment and the collection that you want to run, and click on the "Run" button.
- Once the collection has finished running, you can view the error rate for each request in the "Run Summary" tab.
- To set a threshold for error rate, you can use the industry standard values, which is

typically less than 1%. However, this can vary based on the type of API and the criticality of the requests. For example, an API that performs financial transactions should have a lower error rate than an API that displays news articles.

Sample Program to Detect Error Rate Exceeding 1%

The given below is an example of Python code to check if the error rate is higher than the threshold and print an error message if it is:

```python
import requests

response = requests.get('https://your-api-endpoint.com')
if response.status_code != 200:
    error_rate = 1  # set the error rate threshold as 1%
    if (1 - (response.status_code / response.elapsed.total_seconds())) * 100 > error_rate:
        print("Error: Error Rate exceeded threshold")
```

In the above sample program, if the error rate exceeds the threshold of 1%, an error message is printed.

Identifying Lower Throughput

To identify performance issues related to throughput in Postman, you can use the Collection Runner to run multiple requests simultaneously and measure the number of requests per second.

Below are the steps on how you can do this:
- Open your collection in Postman and click on the "Runner" button in the top-right corner.
- Select the environment and the collection that you want to run, and click on the "Run" button.
- Once the collection has finished running, you can view the number of requests per second in the "Run Summary" tab.
- To set a threshold for throughput, you can use the expected number of requests per second for your API. This can vary based on the nature of your API and the expected traffic volume. You can also compare your throughput with industry benchmarks for similar APIs.

Sample Program to Detect Throughput Below 10 Requests/sec

The given below is an example to check if the throughput is lower than the threshold and print an error message if it is:

```python
import requests
import time

start_time = time.time()
for i in range(100):
    response = requests.get('https://your-api-endpoint.com')
end_time = time.time()

total_time = end_time - start_time
requests_per_second = 100 / total_time
threshold = 10  # set the threshold in requests per second
if requests_per_second < threshold:
    print("Error: Throughput below threshold")
```

In the above sample program, if the throughput is lower than the threshold of 10 requests per second, an error message is printed.

Monitoring CPU and Memory Utilization

To identify performance issues related to CPU and memory utilization in Postman, you can use monitoring tools like New Relic or Datadog. These tools provide detailed metrics on CPU and memory usage, as well as other performance indicators.

To set a threshold for CPU and memory utilization, you can use the recommended guidelines for your server or cloud environment. For example, AWS recommends that CPU utilization should be below 70% for optimal performance, while memory utilization should be below 80%.

Checking Network Latency

To identify performance issues related to network latency in Postman, you can use the Collection Runner to run multiple requests simultaneously and measure the round-trip time for each request.

Below ae steps on how you can do this:

Open your collection in Postman and click on the "Runner" button in the top-right corner. Select the environment and the collection that you want to run, and click on the "Run" button.
Once the collection has finished running, you can view the round-trip time for each request in the "Run Summary" tab.
To set a threshold for network latency, you can use the recommended guidelines for your network infrastructure. For example, Google recommends that network latency should be below 100 milliseconds for optimal user experience.

Sample Program to Notify Latency Exceeding 100ms

The given below is an example to check if the network latency is higher than the threshold and print an error message if it is:

```python
import os

hostname = 'your-api-endpoint.com'
response = os.system("ping -c 1 " + hostname)
threshold = 100  # set the threshold in milliseconds
if response > threshold:
    print("Error: Network Latency exceeded threshold")
```

In the above sample program, if the network latency exceeds the threshold of 100 milliseconds, an error message is printed.

Overall, setting thresholds for performance indicators is critical for identifying performance issues of APIs. By using tools like Postman and monitoring tools, you can track these indicators and measure them against the established thresholds. If the indicators exceed the thresholds, you can take corrective actions to optimize the performance of your API.

Solve and Optimize API Performance

If the performance thresholds are hit, it's important to take corrective actions to rectify and optimize the performances of the APIs.. Improvising API performance requires a combination of techniques, including optimizing the API code, improving the API architecture, using caching, and monitoring and optimizing the API.

Optimize API Code

Optimizing your API code means writing efficient code that reduces the response time and improves the throughput.

Following are some ways to optimize your API code:
- Reduce the number of database queries by using efficient SQL statements and minimizing joins.
- Use pagination to limit the amount of data returned in each request and reduce the load on the server.
- Use caching to store frequently accessed data in memory and reduce the number of requests to the server.

The given below is an example of how to use caching in Python to store frequently accessed data in memory:

```python
import requests
import time

cache = {}

def get_data_from_api(key):
    if key not in cache:
        response = requests.get('https://your-api-endpoint.com/data/' + key)
        cache[key] = response.json()
    return cache[key]

start_time = time.time()
data = get_data_from_api('key1')
end_time = time.time()

response_time = end_time - start_time
```

```python
print("Response Time: ", response_time)
```

In the above sample program, the get_data_from_api function checks if the requested data is in the cache. If it's not in the cache, it sends a request to the API endpoint and stores the data in the cache. If it's in the cache, it returns the data directly from the cache. By using caching, you can significantly reduce the response time and improve the throughput of your API.

Improve API Architecture

Improving your API architecture means designing your API in a way that reduces the response time and improves the throughput.

Following are some ways to improve your API architecture:
- Use a load balancer to distribute the traffic across multiple servers and reduce the load on each server.
- Use a content delivery network (CDN) to cache frequently accessed content and reduce the network latency.
- Use asynchronous processing to reduce the response time and improve the throughput.

The given below is an example of how to use asynchronous processing in Python to improve the response time of your API:

```python
import requests
import asyncio
import time

async def get_data_from_api():
    response = await asyncio.get_event_loop().run_in_executor(None,
requests.get, 'https://your-api-endpoint.com/data/')
    return response.json()

start_time = time.time()
loop = asyncio.get_event_loop()
data = loop.run_until_complete(get_data_from_api())
end_time = time.time()
```

```
response_time = end_time - start_time
print("Response Time: ", response_time)
```

In the above sample program, the get_data_from_api function uses asyncio to send a request to the API endpoint asynchronously. This allows other requests to be processed while waiting for the response from the API endpoint, reducing the response time and improving the throughput of your API.

Use Caching

Using caching means storing frequently accessed data or content in memory or on disk to reduce the number of requests to the server.

The given below are some ways to use caching:
- Use in-memory caching to store frequently accessed data in memory and reduce the response time.
- Use browser caching to cache static content on the client side and reduce the load on the server.
- Use cache expiration to ensure that the cached data is always up-to-date.

The given below is an example of how to use in-memory caching in Python to store frequently accessed data in memory:

```
import requests
import time
import functools

# Define a cache dictionary to store data
cache = {}

# Define a function to retrieve data from the API
def get_data_from_api(key):
    # Check if data is already in cache
    if key in cache:
        print("Retrieving data from cache...")
```

```python
    return cache[key]

    # If data is not in cache, retrieve it from API endpoint
    print("Retrieving data from API...")
    response = requests.get('https://your-api-endpoint.com/data/' + key)

    # Store data in cache
    cache[key] = response.json()

    return cache[key]

# Call the function multiple times with the same key to demonstrate caching
start_time = time.time()
for i in range(5):
    data = get_data_from_api('key1')
end_time = time.time()

response_time = end_time - start_time
print("Response Time: ", response_time)
```

In the above sample program, the get_data_from_api function first checks if the requested data is already in the cache dictionary. If the data is already in the cache, it is immediately returned and the API is not called. If the data is not in the cache, the API is called to retrieve the data and the data is stored in the cache for future use.

Monitor and Optimize

Monitoring your API performance means keeping track of the performance metrics and identifying performance issues.

Following are some ways to monitor and optimize your API:
- Use monitoring tools to track the performance metrics and identify performance issues.
- Set up alerts for performance thresholds to proactively identify issues.
- Continuously optimize the API code and architecture based on the performance

metrics and user feedback.

The given below is an example of how to use monitoring tools to track the performance metrics of your API:

```python
import requests
import time
import newrelic.agent


newrelic.agent.initialize('newrelic.ini')


@newrelic.agent.background_task()
def get_data_from_api():
    response = requests.get('https://your-api-endpoint.com/data/')
    return response.json()


start_time = time.time()
data = get_data_from_api()
end_time = time.time()


response_time = end_time - start_time
print("Response Time: ", response_time)
```

In the above sample program, we're using New Relic to track the performance metrics of our API. We've added the @newrelic.agent.background_task() decorator to the get_data_from_api function to track its performance. New Relic provides detailed metrics on response time, error rate, throughput, and other performance indicators, allowing you to proactively identify performance issues and optimize your API.

To sum it up, by implementing these techniques, you can significantly improve the performance of your API and provide a better user experience.

Chapter 10: API Governance

Understand API Governance

API governance is a set of principles, practices, and processes that help organizations ensure the consistent, secure, and efficient design, implementation, and management of APIs (Application Programming Interfaces) throughout their lifecycle. As APIs have become a critical component of modern software development, understanding and implementing API governance is essential for any organization that seeks to manage and maintain its APIs effectively. In this section, we will discuss the role of API governance and its benefits in an end-to-end API context.

Role of API Governance

Standardization: API governance provides guidelines for the consistent design and development of APIs, ensuring that they are aligned with the organization's architectural principles and industry best practices. Standardization simplifies API consumption, minimizes technical debt, and improves overall maintainability.

Security: APIs are often the primary means by which systems and applications interact with each other. Therefore, ensuring the security of APIs is critical to protect sensitive data and mitigate potential risks. API governance defines and enforces security policies, such as authentication, authorization, and data protection, to guarantee the safety and integrity of APIs.

Quality: API governance ensures that APIs meet performance, reliability, and scalability requirements. This is achieved by establishing and enforcing quality standards, monitoring API performance, and implementing best practices for error handling, caching, and throttling.

Lifecycle Management: APIs have a lifecycle that includes design, development, testing, deployment, maintenance, and retirement. API governance manages the entire lifecycle by providing guidelines, tools, and processes to ensure seamless transitions between different stages, thus preventing inconsistencies and reducing the risk of issues arising from outdated or deprecated APIs.

Collaboration: API governance fosters a collaborative environment within the organization, enabling cross-functional teams to work together effectively during API development. By providing a centralized repository for API documentation, design artifacts, and other related assets, API governance simplifies knowledge sharing and promotes a culture of continuous learning and improvement.

Compliance: API governance helps organizations adhere to industry standards, regulatory requirements, and legal obligations. By defining and enforcing compliance policies, organizations can mitigate the risk of non-compliance and avoid potential fines, reputational damage, and other consequences.

Benefits of API Governance

Improved API Consistency: API governance promotes the development of consistent APIs, which simplifies their consumption by developers and external partners. Consistency reduces the learning curve and accelerates the integration of APIs into applications.

Enhanced Security: API governance helps organizations protect their APIs from security threats by defining and enforcing security policies. This ensures that APIs are developed and maintained with security best practices in mind, thus reducing the risk of data breaches and cyberattacks.

Higher Quality APIs: By enforcing quality standards and monitoring API performance, API governance ensures that APIs meet the organization's expectations for reliability, performance, and scalability. High-quality APIs lead to better end-user experiences and increased trust in the organization's offerings.

Faster Time to Market: API governance streamlines the API development process by providing clear guidelines, tools, and processes that help teams work more efficiently. This accelerates the delivery of new APIs, allowing organizations to quickly respond to changing market demands and maintain a competitive edge.

Reduced Technical Debt: API governance minimizes technical debt by ensuring that APIs are designed, developed, and maintained following best practices. This reduces the need for extensive refactoring or rework in the future and frees up resources for innovation and growth.

Better Compliance: API governance helps organizations adhere to industry standards and regulatory requirements, reducing the risk of non-compliance and the associated penalties.

Create API Governance Framework

An API governance framework is a structured approach that defines the principles, guidelines, processes, and tools to effectively manage APIs throughout their lifecycle. The framework helps organizations ensure consistency, security, maintainability, and compliance across all APIs. To create an API governance framework for API development, follow these steps:

Define API Governance Objectives

In Postman, start by discussing and documenting your organization's API governance objectives. These objectives may include enhancing security, promoting reusability, improving API quality, or ensuring compliance with industry standards and regulations. To document these objectives, you can use Postman's documentation feature. Create a new collection for your API governance framework and add a "Documentation" section to it. In this section, describe your organization's goals related to APIs and the desired outcomes. This documentation will serve as a reference point for your team, helping them understand the purpose and benefits of implementing API governance within your organization.

By defining clear objectives, you set the foundation for your API governance framework in Postman, ensuring that your team has a shared understanding of what you aim to achieve through effective API management.

Establish Principles and Guidelines

Using Postman, establish a set of principles and guidelines that will guide the design, development, and maintenance of APIs. Create a new folder within your API governance collection to store these principles and guidelines. Develop a document outlining API design conventions such as naming conventions, URL structures, and data formats. You may also want to include guidelines for versioning strategies, error handling, and documentation best practices.

Additionally, create templates for API requests and responses within your governance collection. These templates can be used by your team members as a starting point when designing new APIs, ensuring consistency and adherence to established guidelines.

Implement Processes and Workflows

To implement processes and workflows in Postman, first, define the roles and responsibilities of different team members and stakeholders involved in the API development process. Create a document within your API governance collection outlining these roles and their associated responsibilities. Next, establish workflows for each stage of the API development lifecycle. Utilize Postman's collaboration features, such as workspaces, to create separate environments for API design, development, testing, and production. You can also leverage Postman's version control system to manage changes to your API artifacts throughout their lifecycle.

Additionally, set up a process for reviewing and approving API changes. You can use Postman's pull request feature to facilitate this process, allowing team members to submit proposed changes for review and approval by designated approvers.

Choose Appropriate Tools and Technologies

Although Postman offers a wide range of built-in tools for API design, development, and testing, you may need to integrate additional tools and technologies to support your API governance framework fully. Create a document within your API governance collection that lists the chosen tools and technologies, along with their intended purpose and instructions for use. This document will serve as a reference guide for your team members when working with these tools.

Ensure that any external tools and technologies you choose integrate seamlessly with Postman. For example, you might integrate a version control system like GitHub or GitLab with Postman, allowing your team to manage API artifacts directly from the Postman interface.

Define Security and Compliance Policies

In Postman, create a document within your API governance collection that outlines your organization's security and compliance policies. This document should cover aspects such as authentication, authorization, data protection, and auditing. To implement these policies, use Postman's features to define and enforce security best practices within your APIs. For example, you can configure authentication schemes for your APIs using Postman's built-in support for various authentication methods, such as OAuth2 and API keys.

Additionally, create and share a set of pre-defined Postman environment variables containing sensitive information like API keys, ensuring that your team members can access these credentials securely without exposing them in API requests or responses.

Setup Performance Metrics and Monitoring

In Postman, define performance metrics and Key Performance Indicators (KPIs) to measure the success of your API governance framework. These metrics may include API response time, error rates, availability, and adoption rates. To track these metrics in Postman, leverage the monitoring feature to create and schedule monitors for your APIs. These monitors can periodically test your APIs against predefined criteria, such as response times and error rates. You can also set up notifications to alert you if an API fails to meet the specified thresholds, enabling you to identify and address issues proactively.

Additionally, you can use Postman's reporting and analytics features to visualize your API performance data. Generate reports and dashboards that provide insights into API usage, trends, and potential bottlenecks, helping your team make data-driven decisions to improve your APIs and ensure they meet your governance objectives.

Provide Training and Support

To provide training and support on your API governance framework, utilize Postman's extensive documentation and learning resources. Create a folder within your API governance collection dedicated to training materials, including detailed guides, tutorials, and examples that demonstrate how to apply the principles, guidelines, and processes defined in your framework. Additionally, use Postman's collaboration features, such as workspaces and comments, to facilitate knowledge sharing and communication among team members. Encourage your team to ask questions, provide feedback, and contribute to the ongoing improvement of your API governance framework.

Lastly, consider organizing workshops, webinars, or training sessions to help your team members better understand and adopt your API governance framework. These sessions can be tailored to specific roles, such as developers, testers, or product managers, to ensure that each team member has the necessary skills and knowledge to contribute effectively to API governance.

Review and Iterate

Regularly review and evaluate the effectiveness of your API governance framework in Postman. Use the performance metrics and KPIs you've established to analyze your APIs' performance, identify trends, and pinpoint areas for improvement. Gather feedback from your team members and stakeholders on the framework's usability, effectiveness, and areas for potential enhancement. Utilize Postman's collaboration features, such as comments and team discussions, to facilitate open dialogue and encourage a culture of continuous improvement.

Periodically update your API governance documentation, principles, guidelines, and processes to ensure they remain relevant and aligned with your organization's evolving objectives and industry best practices. By continuously reviewing and iterating on your API governance framework, you can ensure it remains effective and adaptable, helping your organization consistently deliver high-quality, secure, and maintainable APIs.

By following these steps and creating a comprehensive API governance framework, your organization can effectively manage APIs throughout their lifecycle, ensuring consistency, security, maintainability, and compliance. This will ultimately lead to higher-quality APIs, improved collaboration, and a faster time to market for new API-driven products and services.

Implement API Governance

Define API Governance Objectives

When defining API governance objectives, it's crucial to involve all relevant stakeholders, including developers, product managers, security experts, and business leaders. This ensures a comprehensive understanding of the organization's needs, priorities, and expectations.

Identify key stakeholders: Start by identifying the main stakeholders involved in the API development process. These stakeholders will provide valuable insights into the objectives and requirements of your API governance framework.

Conduct workshops and interviews: Organize workshops, interviews, or brainstorming sessions with stakeholders to gather their input and perspectives on the API governance objectives. Encourage open discussions and make sure to capture and document their feedback.

Categorize objectives: Categorize the objectives into different areas, such as security, reusability, performance, compliance, and maintainability. This will help you prioritize and focus on the most critical aspects of API governance.

Prioritize objectives: Assess the relative importance of each objective based on factors such as business impact, technical feasibility, and stakeholder requirements. Assign a priority level to each objective, which will help you allocate resources and focus on the most crucial aspects of API governance.

Set measurable goals: For each objective, set measurable goals that can be tracked and evaluated over time. These goals should be Specific, Measurable, Achievable, Relevant, and Time-bound (SMART). For example, a goal related to API security could be: "Implement OAuth2 authentication for all APIs by the end of Q2."

Document objectives and goals: In Postman, create a new collection dedicated to your API governance framework. Add a "Documentation" section and describe the objectives, goals, and priorities you've identified during this process. This documentation will serve as a reference point for your team and help them understand the purpose and benefits of implementing API governance.

Communicate objectives and goals: Share the documented objectives and goals with your team and other stakeholders. Make sure they understand the importance of API governance and how it aligns with the organization's strategic goals.

Schedule regular reviews: Set up a schedule for regular reviews of your API governance objectives and goals. This will help you track progress, identify any deviations or obstacles, and make adjustments as needed.

Establish Principles and Guidelines

After defining your API governance objectives, the next step is to establish a set of principles and guidelines to direct the design, development, and maintenance of your APIs.

Research best practices: Begin by researching industry best practices for API design, development, and management. Consult resources such as API style guides, industry standards, and technical articles. Use this research to inform your API governance principles and guidelines.

Define API design principles: Establish principles for API design, focusing on aspects such as consistency, simplicity, and scalability. These principles should guide your team in designing APIs that are easy to understand, use, and maintain. Examples of API design principles include using consistent naming conventions, preferring RESTful architecture, and using standard HTTP methods and status codes.

Develop API development guidelines: Create guidelines for API development, covering topics such as versioning, error handling, and documentation. These guidelines should help your team build APIs that are reliable, maintainable, and easy to integrate. For example, you might recommend using semantic versioning for API releases, providing detailed error messages, and documenting APIs using the OpenAPI Specification.

Establish API maintenance and deprecation policies: Define policies for API maintenance, including how to handle bug fixes, performance improvements, and feature additions. Also, create a deprecation policy outlining the process for retiring outdated or unused APIs. These policies will ensure that your APIs remain up-to-date, secure, and performant, while minimizing disruptions to consumers.

Create API templates and examples: Develop API request and response templates that adhere to your design principles and guidelines. These templates will serve as a starting point for your team when designing new APIs, promoting consistency and adherence to best practices. Additionally, create examples of well-designed APIs to help your team better understand and apply the principles and guidelines.

Document principles and guidelines: In Postman, create a new folder within your API governance collection to store your principles and guidelines. Develop a document outlining the principles and guidelines you've established, along with any relevant examples or templates. This documentation will serve as a reference guide for your team members as they design, develop, and maintain APIs.

Provide training and support: Organize training sessions or workshops to familiarize your team with the API governance principles and guidelines. Use these sessions to address any questions or concerns and ensure that everyone understands the expectations and best practices for API development.

Implement peer review and approval processes: Encourage your team to review each other's work, ensuring adherence to the principles and guidelines. Set up a process for submitting API designs for review and approval before moving on to development. In Postman, you can use the pull request feature to facilitate this process, allowing team members to submit proposed changes for review and approval by designated approvers.

Monitor and enforce compliance: Regularly review your APIs to ensure compliance with your principles and guidelines. Use Postman's built-in tools, such as the API schema validation and test scripts, to automate this process. Identify and address any deviations or inconsistencies, and provide feedback to help your team improve their API development practices.

Review and update principles and guidelines: Schedule periodic reviews of your API governance principles and guidelines. Gather feedback from your team, analyze industry trends and best practices, and make updates as needed. By keeping your principles and guidelines up-to-date, you can ensure that your APIs continue to meet the evolving needs of your organization and its consumers.

Implement Processes and Workflows

Implementing processes and workflows in your API governance framework is crucial for streamlining the API development lifecycle and promoting collaboration among team members.

Define roles and responsibilities: Begin by outlining the roles and responsibilities of different team members involved in the API development process. These roles may include developers, testers, product managers, and security experts. Ensure that each role's responsibilities are clearly defined and communicated.

Establish development stages: Break down the API development lifecycle into distinct stages, such as design, development, testing, and deployment. This will help your team understand the progression of an API from conception to production and ensure that each stage is properly executed.

Set up collaboration environments: Utilize Postman's workspaces feature to create separate environments for each stage of the API development lifecycle. These environments allow your team to collaborate on API design, development, and testing without affecting the production environment.

Integrate version control: Leverage Postman's integration with version control systems like Git to manage changes to your API artifacts throughout their lifecycle. This will help your team track revisions, compare differences, and ensure that only approved changes are merged and deployed.

Implement review and approval processes: Establish a process for reviewing and approving changes to your APIs before they are promoted to the next stage of the development lifecycle. In Postman, you can use the pull request feature to facilitate this process, allowing team members to submit changes for review and approval by designated approvers.

Define testing procedures: Develop a comprehensive testing strategy for your APIs, including unit testing, functional testing, and performance testing. Use Postman's built-in testing capabilities to create and automate test scripts, ensuring that your APIs meet your quality and performance standards.

Implement monitoring and analytics: Set up monitoring and analytics tools to track the performance and usage of your APIs in production. In Postman, you can use the monitoring feature to schedule automated tests and monitor API response times, error rates, and availability. Configure alerts and notifications to keep your team informed of any issues or anomalies.

Establish API retirement processes: Define a process for retiring outdated or unused APIs, ensuring that they are decommissioned in a controlled and orderly manner. This process should include steps for notifying API consumers, updating documentation, and removing the API from your infrastructure.

Document processes and workflows: In Postman, create a new folder within your API governance collection to store your processes and workflows. Develop a document outlining each stage of the API development lifecycle, the roles and responsibilities of team members, and the tools and techniques used at each stage.

Train and support your team: Provide training and support to your team members on the processes and workflows defined in your API governance framework. Encourage open communication and collaboration, and foster a culture of continuous improvement.

Develop Tools and Automation

Leveraging tools and automation is essential for ensuring consistency, reducing manual effort, and improving the efficiency of your API governance framework.

Utilize Postman's built-in tools: Postman offers a comprehensive suite of tools for API design, development, testing, and monitoring. Use these tools to facilitate collaboration, streamline the API development lifecycle, and automate critical tasks, such as testing and monitoring.

Integrate external tools: Integrate external tools and services, such as version control systems, CI/CD pipelines, and API gateways, to enhance your API governance capabilities. Postman's extensive integration options enable you to connect with a wide range of tools, streamlining your processes and workflows.

Automate testing: Develop test scripts using Postman's built-in testing capabilities to automate the testing of your APIs. Create tests that cover various aspects, such as functionality, performance, and security, ensuring that your APIs meet your quality and performance standards.

Implement monitoring and alerting: Use Postman's monitoring feature to periodically test your APIs against predefined criteria, such as response times and error rates. Configure alerts and notifications to keep your team informed of any issues or anomalies, allowing you to proactively address potential problems.

Automate API documentation: Leverage Postman's automatic API documentation generation capabilities to maintain up-to-date, accurate documentation for your APIs. This not only reduces the manual effort required to maintain documentation but also ensures that your API consumers have access to the latest information.

Automate API schema validation: Use Postman's schema validation features to automatically validate your API requests and responses against a predefined schema, such as the OpenAPI Specification. This helps ensure consistency and adherence to your API design principles and guidelines.

Automate code generation: Utilize Postman's code generation capabilities to automatically generate client libraries and SDKs for your APIs in various programming languages. This reduces the manual effort required to create and maintain these libraries and ensures that your API consumers have access to consistent, up-to-date resources.

Implement security testing and scanning: Integrate security testing and scanning tools into your API governance framework to automatically identify potential vulnerabilities and ensure that your APIs adhere to your security guidelines. Postman can integrate with various security testing tools, such as OWASP ZAP, to automate security assessments.

Create reusable templates and components: Develop reusable API request and response templates, test scripts, and monitoring configurations to promote consistency and reduce manual effort across your APIs. Store these reusable components in your Postman collection to make them easily accessible to your team.

Train your team on tools and automation: Provide training and support to your team members on the tools and automation techniques used in your API governance framework. This will help them understand and adopt the tools effectively and maximize the benefits of automation.

Enforce Compliance and Governance

Enforcing compliance and governance is critical for ensuring that your APIs meet your organization's quality, security, and performance standards, and adhere to industry regulations and standards.

Establish compliance policies: Define policies that outline the regulatory and industry compliance requirements that your APIs must adhere to. These policies should cover aspects such as data privacy, security, and accessibility, depending on your industry and geography.

Develop API contracts: Establish API contracts that outline the terms and conditions for consuming your APIs. These contracts should cover aspects such as usage limits, data ownership, and liability, providing clarity and transparency to your API consumers.

Implement access controls: Use Postman's built-in access control features to manage who has access to your APIs and what actions they can perform. Set up roles and permissions for different user groups, ensuring that only authorized users can access and modify your APIs.

Monitor and audit API activity: Monitor and audit API activity to ensure compliance with your policies and contracts. Use Postman's monitoring and analytics features to track API usage, identify anomalies and potential violations, and generate audit trails.

Implement version control: Use version control systems like Git to manage changes to your API artifacts and track revisions. This helps you maintain a historical record of changes, identify the source of potential issues or violations, and roll back changes if needed.

Conduct compliance testing: Develop compliance tests using Postman's testing capabilities to ensure that your APIs meet your regulatory and industry compliance requirements. Test for aspects such as data privacy, security, and accessibility, identifying any deviations or non-compliant behavior.

Establish incident response processes: Develop processes for responding to incidents, such as security breaches, data breaches, and downtime. These processes should include steps for notification, escalation, and resolution, ensuring that incidents are addressed quickly and effectively.

Conduct regular compliance reviews: Schedule regular reviews of your APIs to ensure ongoing compliance with your policies and contracts. Gather feedback from your team, analyze industry trends and best practices, and make updates as needed.

Provide compliance training: Provide training and support to your team members on compliance policies and regulations relevant to your APIs. Ensure that they understand the importance of compliance and are equipped with the knowledge and skills to adhere to regulatory and industry standards.

Conduct compliance audits: Conduct periodic compliance audits to ensure that your APIs meet regulatory and industry standards. Use Postman's monitoring and analytics features to generate compliance reports and identify areas for improvement.

Continuously Improvise

Continuous improvement is a critical aspect of any API governance framework. By regularly evaluating and improving your processes, tools, and governance policies, you can ensure that your APIs remain relevant, secure, and performant, and continue to meet the evolving needs of your organization and its consumers.

Collect and analyze feedback: Collect feedback from your API consumers and team members, and analyze it to identify areas for improvement. Use Postman's feedback and collaboration features to gather input and suggestions, and incorporate them into your API governance framework.

Measure and track performance: Use Postman's monitoring and analytics features to measure and track the performance and usage of your APIs. Analyze the data to identify areas for improvement, such as response times, error rates, and usage patterns.

Conduct regular reviews: Schedule regular reviews of your API governance framework to identify areas for improvement. Analyze the effectiveness of your processes, tools, and policies, and make updates as needed.

Incorporate industry best practices: Stay up-to-date with industry trends and best practices, and incorporate them into your API governance framework. Attend industry events and conferences, read industry publications, and participate in industry forums to stay informed.

Conduct internal audits: Conduct periodic internal audits to ensure that your APIs meet your organization's quality, security, and performance standards. Use Postman's testing and monitoring capabilities to identify areas for improvement and implement corrective actions.

Foster a culture of innovation: Foster a culture of innovation and experimentation within your team, encouraging them to try new approaches and technologies to improve your API governance practices.

Continuously train and upskill your team: Provide ongoing training and support to your team members to ensure that they stay up-to-date with the latest API governance practices, technologies, and industry trends.

Implement continuous integration and delivery: Use continuous integration and delivery (CI/CD) pipelines to automate the testing, deployment, and delivery of your APIs. This helps you reduce manual effort, accelerate delivery, and improve the quality and reliability of your APIs.

Develop a roadmap: Develop a roadmap for the evolution of your API governance framework, outlining the planned updates, improvements, and new initiatives. Use Postman's collections and workspaces features to store and track your roadmap, making it easily accessible to your team.

Celebrate successes: Celebrate the successes of your API governance framework, recognizing the achievements of your team members and API consumers. This helps foster a positive and collaborative culture, motivating your team to continue improving your API governance practices.

Overall, implementing an effective API governance framework is critical for managing APIs throughout their lifecycle, ensuring consistency, security, maintainability, and compliance. By following the six key steps outlined above, you can develop an API governance framework that meets your organization's needs and maximizes the value of your APIs. Through defining objectives, developing design principles and guidelines, implementing processes and workflows, developing tools and automation, enforcing compliance and governance, and continuously improving, you can establish a comprehensive and effective API governance framework in Postman. By leveraging Postman's features and integrations, you can streamline your API development lifecycle, promote collaboration and communication among team members, and ensure that your APIs meet your organization's quality, security, and performance standards. Overall, implementing an API governance framework is a critical step for any organization looking to establish a successful API program. With Postman's powerful tools and features, you can establish a robust and effective API governance framework that maximizes the value of your APIs, improves your organization's agility and flexibility, and drives innovation and growth.

Managing API Policies and Standards

Managing API policies and standards in Postman involves establishing policies and guidelines, setting up automated checks and validations, and monitoring API usage to ensure compliance. Following are the detailed steps you can follow to manage API policies and standards in Postman:

Define Policies and Guidelines

Define policies and guidelines for API development, such as data privacy, security, and accessibility, and establish API contracts that outline the terms and conditions for consuming your APIs. Use Postman's documentation feature to create and maintain up-to-date, accurate documentation for your APIs, outlining your policies and guidelines.

Steps to define policies and guidelines:
1. Open the Postman app and navigate to the documentation tab.
2. Create a new documentation page or update an existing one with your policies and guidelines for API development.
3. Include information such as data privacy, security, accessibility, and API contracts that outline the terms and conditions for consuming your APIs.

Setting Up Automated Checks and Validations

Use Postman's built-in validation capabilities to implement automated checks for adherence to your policies and guidelines. For example, you can use Postman's schema validation feature to validate requests and responses against a predefined schema, such as the OpenAPI Specification. This ensures consistency and adherence to your API design principles and guidelines.

Steps to set up automated checks and validations:
1. Create a new API request in Postman, and define the request body and response schema using the OpenAPI Specification.
2. Save the API request as part of your collection in Postman.
3. Configure schema validation using the built-in feature in Postman by specifying the OpenAPI Specification schema.
4. Run the validation test to ensure that the request and response adhere to the predefined schema.

Monitor API Usage

Use Postman's monitoring and analytics features to track the performance and usage of your APIs in production. Monitor API response times, error rates, and availability, and configure alerts and notifications to keep your team informed of any issues or anomalies. This allows you to proactively address potential problems and ensure compliance with your policies and guidelines.

Steps to monitor API usage:
1. Use Postman's built-in monitoring feature to periodically test your APIs against predefined criteria such as response times and error rates.
2. Configure alerts and notifications to receive real-time alerts when API performance falls below predefined thresholds.
3. Use the analytics feature to track API usage, response times, and error rates, and identify potential issues or trends in usage patterns.

Conduct Compliance Testing

Develop compliance tests using Postman's testing capabilities to ensure that your APIs meet your regulatory and industry compliance requirements. Test for aspects such as data privacy, security, and accessibility, identifying any deviations or non-compliant behavior.

Steps to conduct compliance testing:
Develop compliance tests using Postman's testing capabilities to ensure that your APIs meet your regulatory and industry compliance requirements.
Test for aspects such as data privacy, security, and accessibility by defining test cases that validate compliance requirements.
Run the compliance tests regularly to ensure ongoing compliance with your policies and guidelines.

Integrate with External Tools

Integrate Postman with external tools and services, such as security scanning tools or API gateways, to enhance your API governance capabilities. For example, you can integrate Postman with OWASP ZAP to automate security assessments and identify potential vulnerabilities.

Steps to integrate with external tools:
1. Integrate Postman with external tools such as security scanning tools or API gateways using the available integrations in Postman.
2. Configure the integration to run security assessments or monitor API traffic for potential threats.
3. Set up alerts and notifications to be notified of potential vulnerabilities or non-compliant behavior.

Enforce Access Controls

Use Postman's access control features to manage who has access to your APIs and what actions they can perform. Set up roles and permissions for different user groups, ensuring that only authorized users can access and modify your APIs.

Step to enforce access controls:
1. Use Postman's access control features to manage who has access to your APIs and what actions they can perform.
2. Set up roles and permissions for different user groups, ensuring that only authorized users can access and modify your APIs.
3. Monitor API access using Postman's analytics feature, and identify any unauthorized access attempts or modifications to your APIs.

By following these steps, you can effectively manage your API policies and standards in Postman, ensuring compliance with your organization's quality, security, and performance standards, and adherence to industry regulations and standards.

CHAPTER 11: ADVANCED API DEVELOPER SKILLS

Understand Variables

Variables in Postman allow developers to store and reuse values within requests and scripts. They can be used to create dynamic requests that can adapt to different scenarios, without having to manually update each request individually. For example, you might use a variable to store an authentication token that is used across multiple requests, or to store a URL that changes depending on the environment.

Variables in Postman are useful for a number of reasons:

1. Reusability: Variables allow you to reuse values across multiple requests, reducing the need for duplication and manual updates.

2. Dynamic requests: By using variables in your requests, you can create dynamic requests that can adapt to different scenarios. For example, you might use a variable to store a URL that changes depending on the environment.

3. Easy management: Variables can be easily managed and updated in Postman, making it easy to make changes to multiple requests at once.

There are two types of variables in Postman: global and local. Global variables are accessible across all requests and environments. A global variable in Postman is a variable that can be accessed and used across all requests and environments in a Postman collection. Global variables are created and managed in the 'Variables' tab of the Postman app, and can be used to store values that are used across multiple requests, such as authentication tokens, endpoints, or other common values. While local variables are specific to a particular request or environment. A local variable in Postman is a variable that is specific to a particular request or environment. Local variables are created and managed within the request builder, and can be used to store values that are unique to each request, such as parameters or headers.

Global variables in Postman are useful for many purposes, including:
* Storing values that are used across multiple requests, such as authentication tokens or endpoints.
* Creating dynamic requests that can adapt to different environments or scenarios.
* Reducing the need for duplication and manual updates.
* Improving the organization and scalability of your API development and testing efforts.

Local variables in Postman are useful for many purposes, including:
* Storing values that are unique to each request, such as parameters or headers.

- Creating dynamic requests that can adapt to different scenarios.
- Reducing the need for duplication and manual updates.
- Improving the organization and scalability of your API development and testing efforts.

Working with Global Variables

Let us try how you can create and work with global variables in Postman:

Create a Global Variable

- Open the Postman app and select the collection in which you want to create the global variable.
- Click on the 'Variables' tab at the top of the screen.
- Click the 'Add' button to create a new global variable.
- Enter a name for the variable, and the initial value you want to assign to it.
- Click 'Save' to create the variable.

Use the Global Variable in a Request

- Open the request in which you want to use the global variable.
- In the request builder, use double curly braces ({{}}) to enclose the name of the global variable.
- For example, if you created a global variable named 'baseUrl', you would use {{baseUrl}} in the request URL or headers.
- When you send the request, Postman will automatically replace the variable placeholder with the value of the global variable.

Update a Global Variable

- Navigate to the 'Variables' tab in the Postman app.
- Locate the global variable you want to update.
- Click the 'Edit' button next to the variable.
- Update the value of the variable, and click 'Save' to save your changes.

Delete a Global Variable

- Navigate to the 'Variables' tab in the Postman app.
- Locate the global variable you want to delete.
- Click the 'Delete' button next to the variable.
- Confirm that you want to delete the variable.

Using Local Variables

Let us try this as well on how you can create and work with local variables in Postman:

Create a Local Variable

- Open the Postman app and select the request in which you want to create the local variable.
- In the request builder, click on the 'Params' or 'Headers' tab, depending on where you want to use the variable.
- Click the 'Add' button to create a new parameter or header.
- In the 'Key' field, enter the name of the local variable, enclosed in double curly braces ({{}}).
- For example, if you want to create a local variable named 'apiKey', you would enter {{apiKey}} in the 'Key' field.
- In the 'Value' field, enter the initial value you want to assign to the variable.
- Click 'Save' to create the variable.

Use the Local Variable in the Request

- In the request builder, use double curly braces ({{}}) to enclose the name of the local variable wherever you want to use it. For example, if you created a local variable named 'apiKey', you would use {{apiKey}} in the URL or headers of the request.
- When you send the request, Postman will automatically replace the variable placeholder with the value of the local variable.

Update a Local Variable

- Open the request in which you want to update the local variable.
- In the request builder, locate the parameter or header that contains the local variable you want to update.
- Update the value of the local variable.
- Click 'Save' to save your changes.

Delete a Local Variable

- Open the request in which you want to delete the local variable.
- In the request builder, locate the parameter or header that contains the local variable you want to delete.
- Delete the local variable from the 'Key' field.
- Click 'Save' to save your changes.

Understand Environments

Environments in Postman allow developers to manage sets of variables that are specific to a particular environment, such as development, staging, or production. Environments are used to store values that are unique to each environment, such as different API keys, endpoints, or credentials.

Environments in Postman are useful for several reasons:
- Organization: Environments allow you to organize sets of variables by environment, making it easier to manage and update values that are specific to each environment.
- Scalability: Environments make it easier to scale your API development and testing efforts, by allowing you to manage different sets of variables for different environments.
- Consistency: By using environments to manage sets of variables, you can ensure that requests and tests are consistent across different environments, reducing the risk of errors and improving overall quality.

Administering Environments

To administer environments in Postman, follow these steps:

Open Postman:
Launch the Postman application on your computer.

Create a new environment:
In the top right corner of the Postman app, click on the gear icon, which will open the "Manage Environments" modal. Click on the "Add" button to create a new environment. Give your environment a name, such as "Development" or "Production."

Add key-value pairs:
In the new environment, you can add key-value pairs that represent the variables you want to use in your requests. For example, if you have a base URL that changes between environments, you could add a key called "base_url" and set its value to the appropriate URL for this environment.

Example:

Key: base_url

Value: https://api-dev.example.com

Save the environment:
Click the "Add" button at the bottom of the modal to save your new environment.

Switch between environments:
You can now switch between environments using the dropdown menu in the top right corner of the Postman app. This will automatically update the values of the variables used in your requests.

Use environment variables in requests:
To use an environment variable in a request, wrap the key in double curly braces {{ }}. For example, if you have a variable called "base_url", you could use it in your request like this:

GET {{base_url}}/endpoint

When you switch between environments, Postman will automatically replace the {{base_url}} placeholder with the corresponding value from the selected environment.

Update environment variables:
If you need to update the value of an environment variable, go back to the "Manage Environments" modal by clicking on the gear icon, then click on the environment you want to edit. Update the value of the variable and click "Update" to save your changes.

To sum it up, variables and environments are powerful features in Postman that can greatly improve the efficiency and effectiveness of the API lifecycle. By using variables and environments, developers can create dynamic requests, reuse values across multiple requests, and manage sets of variables for different environments. This can improve organization, scalability, and consistency, and reduce the risk of errors and improve overall quality.

Automate API Testing

Automating API testing in Postman can be done using the "Collections Runner" or the command-line tool "Newman". In this explanation, we'll cover both methods.

Creating Collection

First, you need to organize your API requests into a collection. A collection is a group of related requests that can be executed together.
Proceed with the following steps:
- In the Postman app, click on the "Collections" tab on the left sidebar.
- Click on the "Create a collection" button (a folder icon with a plus sign).
- Give your collection a name and description, then click "Create".

Now you can add requests to your collection by clicking the "Add requests" button within the collection, or by dragging existing requests from your workspace into the collection.

Writing Tests

For each request in your collection, you can write tests using JavaScript in the "Tests" tab.
Proceed with the following steps:
- Select a request in your collection.
- Click on the "Tests" tab in the request panel.
- Write your tests using Postman's built-in pm.test() function and the pm.* API.

Example:
Test JSON response with a status code of 200:

```
pm.test("Status code is 200", function () {
    pm.response.to.have.status(200);
});


pm.test("Response is JSON", function () {
    pm.response.to.be.json;
});
```

Running Tests with Collections Runner

Click on the "Runner" button at the top left of the Postman app.

In the Collections Runner window, select the collection you want to run from the "Collection" dropdown.

Choose the environment (if any) from the "Environment" dropdown.

Click the "Run" button to start running your tests. The test results will be displayed in the "Run Results" tab.

Automating Tests using Newman

Newman is a command-line tool that enables you to run your Postman collections, making it an essential tool for integration into your CI/CD pipeline. With Newman, you can run your tests in an automated and streamlined manner, making it an ideal choice for continuous integration and delivery. This tool provides a simple and efficient way to test your APIs, making it a valuable addition to your testing arsenal. Additionally, Newman allows you to generate custom HTML reports, making it easier to analyze your test results and communicate your findings to other members of your team.

Install Newman using npm (Node.js package manager):

```
npm install -g newman
```

Export your collection and environment (if any) as JSON files:
- In Postman, right-click on your collection and select "Export". Choose the export format as "Collection v2.1" and save the file.
- If you have an environment, click the gear icon at the top right corner, click on the environment, and select "Download" to export it as a JSON file.

Run your tests using Newman:

```
newman run <path_to_collection_file> -e <path_to_environment_file>
```

Replace <path_to_collection_file> with the path to your exported collection JSON file and <path_to_environment_file> with the path to your exported environment JSON file (if you have one).

Newman will run your tests and display the results in the command-line interface.

By following these steps, you can automate your API testing in Postman and use it as part of your continuous integration and deployment processes.

Automate Deployment using GitHub Actions

To automate API deployment in Postman using GitHub Actions, you can set up a CI/CD pipeline that automatically runs your Postman tests using Newman whenever you push changes to your GitHub repository.

Following is a step-by-step directions to automate deployment:

Install Newman and export your collection and environment:
Follow the instructions provided in the previous section to install Newman and export your Postman collection and environment as JSON files.

Create a GitHub repository:
If you haven't already, create a new GitHub repository and clone it to your local machine.

Add your Postman collection and environment files:
Place your exported Postman collection and environment JSON files into your GitHub repository's root directory or a designated folder.

Set up a GitHub Actions workflow:
- In your GitHub repository, create a new folder called ".github" in the root directory.
- Inside the ".github" folder, create another folder called "workflows".
- In the "workflows" folder, create a new YAML file, e.g., "postman_tests.yml".

Configure the GitHub Actions workflow:
Open the "postman_tests.yml" file and configure your GitHub Actions workflow. The given below is an example:

```yaml
name: Postman Tests

on:
  push:
    branches:
      - main

jobs:
```

```yaml
test:
  runs-on: ubuntu-latest

  steps:
  - name: Checkout repository
    uses: actions/checkout@v2

  - name: Set up Node.js
    uses: actions/setup-node@v2
    with:
      node-version: 14

  - name: Install dependencies
    run: npm ci

  - name: Install Newman
    run: npm install -g newman

  - name: Run Postman tests
    run: newman run <path_to_collection_file> -e <path_to_environment_file>
```

Replace <path_to_collection_file> and <path_to_environment_file> with the paths to your exported collection and environment JSON files, respectively.

This workflow is configured to run on the "main" branch. It checks out your repository, sets up Node.js, installs Newman, and runs your Postman tests using Newman.

Commit and push your changes:
Add your Postman collection, environment files, and GitHub Actions workflow to your repository, then commit and push your changes:

```
git add .
git commit -m "Add Postman tests and GitHub Actions workflow"
```

Monitor your GitHub Actions workflow:
After pushing your changes, navigate to the "Actions" tab in your GitHub repository to see the progress of your GitHub Actions workflow. You can check the logs and test results for each step in the workflow.

By following these steps, you can automate API deployment in Postman using GitHub Actions, ensuring your APIs are tested and validated each time you push changes to your repository.

Writing Custom Scripts in Postman

To become an expert at writing custom scripts in Postman, you'll need to practice and familiarize yourself with the various features and functionalities Postman offers as discussed thus far in this book. Custom scripts in Postman are written in JavaScript and can be used for pre-request scripts or tests.

The given below is a step-by-step walkthrough to help you develop this skill:
- Understand JavaScript: To write custom scripts in Postman, you need a strong understanding of JavaScript. If you're not already familiar with JavaScript, there are numerous resources available online, such as Mozilla Developer Network (MDN), freeCodeCamp, and W3Schools, to help you learn.
- Learn Postman Basics: Familiarize yourself with the basic features of Postman, such as creating requests, managing collections, and using environments. Understanding these basics will help you write effective custom scripts. If you have come so far, then you must have learned the required skill set of using Postman.
- Explore Postman Scripting API: Postman provides a scripting API called pm.* that allows you to interact with various aspects of your requests, responses, and environment. Study the official Postman documentation for the pm.* API and understand its different methods and properties. Some important ones include pm.request, pm.response, pm.environment, pm.variables, and pm.test. These are also covered in the book so you should be good to begin with writing custom scripts.
- Pre-request Scripts: Pre-request scripts are executed before sending a request. They can be used to set up variables, modify request data, or perform calculations. To write a pre-request script, select a request and click on the "Pre-request Script" tab in the request panel. Here, you can write your JavaScript code to manipulate your request data or environment variables.
- Test Scripts: Test scripts are executed after receiving a response. They are used to

validate the response data, check for expected values, or set environment variables. To write a test script, select a request and click on the "Tests" tab in the request panel. Write your JavaScript code using the pm.test() function and the pm.* API to create assertions and validate the response.

- Practice: The key to becoming an expert at writing custom scripts in Postman is practice. Create sample APIs or use existing public APIs to write pre-request scripts and test scripts for various scenarios. As you practice, you'll become more familiar with the pm.* API and improve your scripting skills.
- Collaborate and Learn from Others: Join the Postman community and participate in discussions, ask questions, and share your knowledge. Learning from others' experiences and sharing your own will help you develop expert skills in writing custom scripts in Postman.

By following these steps and dedicating time to practice and exploration, you can develop expert skills in writing custom scripts in Postman and significantly enhance your API development and testing capabilities. Check below on some examples to write custom scripts in postman.

Sample Custom Script: Generating Timestamp & Setting Environment Variable

```
const timestamp = Date.now();
pm.environment.set("current_timestamp", timestamp);
```

Sample Custom Script: Testing JSON Response for Specific Value

```
pm.test("Check if response has user ID 1", function () {
    const jsonData = pm.response.json();
    pm.expect(jsonData.id).to.equal(1);
});
```

Postman Best Practices

1. Make use of meaningful names and descriptions: Provide your requests, collections, and folders with names that are descriptive, and include pertinent information in the descriptions of those items. This makes it easier for you and your team to quickly understand the purpose of each item as well as how it functions.
2. Create collections and folders to organize your API requests as follows: Create collections of API requests that are related to one another, and then use folders to

further organize them. This contributes to the maintenance of a well-structured workspace, which in turn makes it much simpler to locate and manage requests.

3. Utilize environment variables: Make use of environment variables to store configuration data, such as base URLs, API keys, and access tokens, since these are the kinds of things that can vary depending on the environment (e.g., development, staging, and production). Because of this, switching between environments can be accomplished with less effort and without requiring individual requests to be modified.

4. Utilize global variables: Make use of global variables for data that must be shared across all requests and environments. When using them, however, you should exercise extreme caution because, if they are not managed correctly, they can inadvertently have an effect on other requests.

5. Collaborate on the creation of collections and environments with your team by using shared workspaces to share and discuss the environments and collections you've created. This ensures that everyone is working with the same data and configurations by providing a unified source of information.

6. Postman templates should be created: To save time and ensure that all of your API requests are processed in the same manner, you should create templates for the most frequently used request structures, such as authentication and pagination.

7. Use pre-request scripts: Write pre-request scripts to set up or manipulate request data before sending requests. The creation of timestamps, the setting of headers, and the calculation of values are all potential applications for this.

8. Write test scripts: Develop test scripts for every request in order to validate response data, status codes, and other aspects of your application programming interface (API). This makes it easier to spot errors and inconsistencies in your API and helps to ensure that it behaves as expected.

9. Leverage the Postman pm.* API: When working with requests, responses, and variables in scripts, it is helpful to leverage the Postman pm.* API. This application programming interface (API) offers a potent toolkit for interacting with API data and validating it.

10. Utilize Postman's built-in code snippets: Postman provides built-in code snippets for common test scenarios, such as checking status codes or parsing JSON. These built-in code snippets can be used to accomplish a variety of tasks. Make use of these snippets so that you can write test scripts more quickly.

11. Maintain regular updates for Postman: Maintaining an up-to-date version of the Postman application allows you to take advantage of newly added features, bug fixes, and improvements in performance.

12. Import/export collections and environments: Make backups, share environments, and transfer collections by utilizing the import/export feature that is available in Postman. This helps to maintain consistency across all devices and members of the team.

13. Configure request timeouts and retries: In order to prevent unneeded delays or failures in your tests, it is important to configure request timeouts and retries for APIs that are unreliable or slow.

14. Make use of authentication settings as well as request headers: Postman includes built-in support for a variety of authentication methods, including OAuth and Basic Auth, which can be used to add required headers and authentication information to API requests.

15. Create mock servers by utilizing the mock server feature that is available in Postman to simulate API response data while you are developing or testing. You are able to construct and test API clients with this without having to rely on live APIs.

16. Utilize Postman as your monitor: Postman monitors allow for the scheduling and automation of API tests. This assists in identifying potential problems before they have an impact on end-users.

17. Postman's API documentation feature allows you to automatically generate and share documentation for your APIs. By using this feature, you can ensure that both your team and the people who use your APIs have access to information that is accurate and up to date.

18. Utilize version control: Postman includes support for version control for collections, which enables you to track changes, create branches, and merge updates, thereby assisting you in maintaining a clear history of your API development.

19. Utilize Postman's Visualizer: The visualizer feature of Postman allows you to display response data in a format that is both easier to read and more visually appealing. This makes it much simpler to comprehend complicated data structures.

20. Postman can be integrated with CI/CD by using Newman: As a component of your continuous integration and deployment pipeline, you can execute Postman scripts with the help of the command-line tool Newman.

21. Take advantage of the Postman Console: Make use of the Postman Console to diagnose issues with requests, scripts, and tests. It displays detailed information about each request, including headers, cookies, and script execution logs, which assists you in identifying problems and finding solutions to them in a timely manner.

22. Perform routine cleanups: Get rid of collections, requests, and variables that aren't being used to keep your workspace organized and clutter-free. This helps ensure that your team is working with the most up-to-date information and reduces the likelihood of confusion occurring.

23. Consider the following examples: Utilizing the examples feature of Postman, you can generate multiple examples for each request. This helps demonstrate various use cases, response formats, and possible error scenarios for your application programming interface (API).

24. Use JSON schema validation: Compare the data received as a response to a JSON

schema in order to check that the structure and data types are accurate. This makes it easier to spot inconsistencies and ensures that your API is compliant with the anticipated schema.

25. Make use of the GraphQL support provided by Postman: You'll have a much easier time working with GraphQL APIs if you use Postman because it comes with built-in support for GraphQL queries and mutations.

26. Utilize dynamic variables: Use Postman's dynamic variables, such as "$randomInt," to generate random data for your requests. This will ensure that your responses are as unique as possible. This assists in the creation of diverse test scenarios and the discovery of potential edge cases.

27. Make use of request chaining, in which you take information from the response of one request and use it in another request by making use of variables. This makes it easier to model intricate workflows as well as the dependencies that exist between API endpoints.

28. Make use of tags to improve your organization: It will be much simpler for you to search and filter your workspace if you apply tags to your requests, collections, and folders.

29. Make use of the collaboration features offered by Postman: To enhance the level of communication and coordination that exists within your team, make use of features such as real-time collaboration, commenting, and activity feeds.

30. Manipulate the cookies: Utilizing Postman's built-in support for cookies, you can manage and manipulate the cookies that are included in your requests.

31. Utilize Postman's scripting libraries: Postman supports a number of JavaScript libraries, such as Lodash, Moment.js, and Ajv, which can improve your ability to script. These libraries are supported by Postman.

32. Utilize the runner for the collection: Using the collection runner, carry out a number of requests and tests. Doing so will assist in locating problems and evaluating the overall performance of the API.

33. Keep an eye on the performance of the API: Utilizing Postman's built-in monitoring tools, you can keep track of response times in addition to other performance metrics.

34. Validate API contracts: Do not forget to check that your application programming interface (API) complies with the agreed-upon standards and requirements by using contract testing.

35. Export data to a variety of formats: Postman enables the exporting of data, such as test results or collection information, to a variety of formats, such as JSON, CSV, or HTML.

36. Make use of the search function: Conduct a search throughout your workspace, collections, and environments to locate and quickly access the requests or variables you are looking for.

37. Utilize the tab labeled history: Examine the request history in order to keep track

of your activity and investigate previous requests.

38. Utilize the keyboard shortcuts: Postman's keyboard shortcuts can help you become more efficient and speed up your workflow if you take the time to learn and use them.

39. Exercise proper handling of errors: Create test scripts to simulate various error conditions, such as incorrect data, invalid responses, and server malfunctions. This contributes to ensuring that your API is both resilient and robust.

40. Utilize Postman's newman-reporter: Utilize newman-reporter to produce individualized HTML reports for your various test runs. This enables you to communicate test results and findings to your team in a more clear and concise manner.

41. Utilize Postman's built-in team collaboration features to improve the efficiency with which you and your colleagues work together, share requests, collections, and environments, and administer team roles and permissions.

42. Postman's Newman Run can be Utilized in Parallel: Reduce the amount of time needed to complete tests by utilizing the parallel running capabilities of Newman Run in Parallel.

43. Use Mock Servers to Design API: Use Postman Mock Server to design API as per the response you would like to receive, this is a great way to understand how your API should work and what it should return, and using Mock Servers to design API is a great way to get started.

44. Utilize Postman's Built-In Authorization Flow Options to Define Your API's Authorization and Scopes Utilize Postman's built-in authorization flow options in order to define your API's authorization and scopes.

45. Utilize Mock Responses: During testing, you can use Postman's mock response feature to return predefined responses; this helps simulate various types of responses and errors.

46. Make use of the Request Body Editor found in Postman. With the help of the Request Body Editor, you can easily create request payloads for your API requests. It provides assistance in the creation of structured payloads that can contain nested objects and arrays.

47. Make use of the Postman API. Postman's built-in API schema support enables you to define and manage the schema for your APIs. You can use this feature to save time.

48. Utilize Collection Sharing: Either generate a link that can be shared with your team in order to share your collections with them, or invite your team members to your workspace in order for them to collaborate.

49. Use of the Collection Runner in Conjunction with Variables Make use of the collection runner in conjunction with variables to test various scenarios in parallel with various sets of data.

50. Utilize Collection Documentation: Make use of the collection documentation

feature offered by Postman in order to generate documentation for your APIs. This can be useful when onboarding new team members or when sharing your APIs with teams from outside your organization.

These best practices include using meaningful names and descriptions for requests, organizing API requests into collections and folders, utilizing environment variables and global variables, and sharing collections and environments with your team using workspaces. Additionally, it is important to use built-in features like pre-request scripts, test scripts, code snippets, request headers and authentication settings, mock servers, and monitors to enhance the efficiency and effectiveness of API development and testing.

Other best practices include regularly updating Postman, importing and exporting collections and environments, using request timeouts and retries, utilizing Postman's visualizer and version control features, and integrating Postman with CI/CD using Newman. It is also essential to handle cookies, use Postman's scripting libraries, and validate API contracts. Postman's collaboration features, keyboard shortcuts, and search and history tabs should also be utilized, along with practicing error handling, using newman-reporter, and working with Mock Servers to design API.

Overall, by following these best practices, API producers can ensure they are getting the most out of Postman and delivering high-quality APIs that meet user needs and expectations.

Thank You

Epilogue

As you close the final pages of "Mastering Postman," you may feel a sense of accomplishment and newfound confidence in your abilities as a developer. Throughout the book, you have learned the ins and outs of using Postman, a powerful tool for working with APIs. You have also discovered the ways in which Excel can be leveraged in conjunction with Postman to streamline your workflow and ensure that your APIs are robust and effective.

But this is not the end of your journey. In fact, it is just the beginning. As you move forward in your career as a developer, you will undoubtedly encounter new challenges and opportunities that will require you to use the skills and knowledge you have gained through mastering Postman.

Perhaps you will find yourself building more complex APIs that require you to work with larger datasets and handle more intricate logic. In these cases, the techniques you have learned for testing and debugging with Postman will be invaluable. You may also need to work with other developers, teams, and stakeholders to coordinate efforts and ensure that your APIs meet the needs of your users. Here, the collaboration and documentation features of Postman will be crucial.

Or, you may find yourself working on projects that require integration with other technologies or platforms. In these cases, you can draw on the Excel skills you have acquired to manipulate and analyze data in a way that complements your API development work. You may also need to explore other tools and frameworks to accomplish your goals, such as Swagger, Insomnia, or SoapUI.

Whatever challenges you may face, you can be confident that the foundation you have built through mastering Postman will serve you well. You now have a deep understanding of how APIs work and how to build and test them effectively. You have also developed a strong set of skills and practices for working collaboratively and iteratively throughout the development lifecycle.

As you look back on your journey, you may feel a sense of pride and satisfaction in all that you have accomplished. But you should also look forward with excitement and curiosity, eager to explore new technologies, collaborate with new colleagues, and tackle new challenges with the confidence and expertise that you have gained through mastering Postman.

Made in the USA
Monee, IL
07 July 2026

56552387R00109